Phil La Duke

Stop.
Don't Shoot!

Preparing for
and Surviving
Mass Shootings
and Rampage Attacks

All rights reserved. No part of this publication may be reproduced, stored in a retrieval system, or transmitted in any form or by any means, electronic, mechanical, photocopying, audio recording, or otherwise, without the prior permission of the publisher or author.

ISBN: 978-1-945853-35-7

Printed by Marriah Publishing

Edition 1

New Jersey, the United States of America

November 30, 2022

Testimonials

"Phil's research into this timely subject is fascinating and much needed. As a nation, we can't seem to be able to have an adult conversation on point. Phil's work should make us all rethink and begin to address the issue."

— **Andrew Arena, Executive Director, Detroit Crime Commission, founder of A.S. Consulting, LLC and former FBI Special Agent In Charge, Head of Counter Terrorism**

"I can't say enough about how important this book is. In today's society the chances of an armed rage attack can't be discounted. Phil LaDuke's style and substance make this book a must read."

—**Jonathan Gold, Michigan Chapter President, Giffords Gun Owners for Safety**

"We can all be thankful that Phil La Duke has applied his lifetime accumulated knowledge of how to prevent workplace accidents to the much darker topic of preventing the "rampage attacks" that have become numbingly routine in America."

— **Peter Page, Editor, The Grit Daily News**

"Phil's writing takes us where we need to go. It's not always where we want to be, or even where we thought we would end up. The tireless amount of research Phil puts into his work coupled with a journalistic integrity that is nearly extinct these days serves up a raw, unflinching look at the state of things as they are now, and what needs to be done to make our world safer, and ultimately better."

— **Jason Maldonado, Co-Host of the Safety Justice League podcast and author of "A Practical Guide to the Safety Profession: The Relentless Pursuit**

"With violence in the workplace becoming more common with multiple dead per incident, it's important to increase knowledge on prevention activities - not just response. Phil's voice is reasonable, practical, helpful, ——————— and hopeful. We can and must do better for our workplaces."

—**Abby Ferri, Chief Risk Officer at Insurate**

Stop. Don't Shoot!

Why?

Image credit: Amy LaDuke

"The silicon chip inside her head gets switched to overload, and nobody's gonna go to school today, she's gonna make them stay at home. And daddy doesn't understand it. He always said she was as good as gold, and he can see no reasons 'cause there are no reasons. What reason to do you need to be shown?"
—"I Don't Like Mondays" Sir Bob Geldoff

When I first started writing this book over two years ago, I was continually asked why people commit mass shootings. Despite much conjecture and conventional wisdom, most of what people believe is just plain wrong. As former FBI Special Agent in Charge assigned to Counter Terrorism Andrew Arena told me in an interview for this book, "Nobody is really sure why some people go on a rampage and commit mass murder." Jonathan Gold Giffords Senior Ambassador and President of Giffords Gun Owners for Michigan, echoes these sentiments, "We can't attribute any cause to mass shootings because we can never truly know what is in the mind of the perpetrator." With that said, we have a pretty good idea of the things that don't hold up to research:

Violent Video Games

In an article published in the July 2015 edition of *Scientific American*, "Do Video Games Inspire Violent Behavior? Conventional Wisdom Suggests Violent Media Is Harming Kids. But Sometimes A Game Is Just A Game," Author Greg Toppo asserts, "The truth is that decades of research have turned up no reliable causal link between playing violent video games and perpetrating actual violence." In fact, Toppo shares the story of the Sandy Hook shooter who was so obsessed with playing a video game at a nearby movie theater—playing 8–10 hours a day—that the manager sometimes had to unplug the game to get the frenzied teen to leave. The game that had him so worked up? Dance Dance Revolution.

The article is well worth the read and has additional key findings, including:

- Children who observe an adult acting violently tend to follow suit when they are frustrated.

- Violent games appear to be effective teachers of aggressive attitudes.

- Research has failed to show a causal relation between playing violent games and perpetrating violent acts.

- The fighting that kids engage in with video games is more akin to play than violence."[1]

This article (and others like it) are infuriating! Of course violent video games cause our sweet, innocent children to become cold-blooded killers. We want to believe that because it's intuitive, it's self-evident, it's…wrong. In his book *Blunder: Why Smart People Make Bad Decisions*, author Zachary Shore introduces several "cognitive blinds" that cause even the smartest among us to make poor assumptions and bad decisions, because the facts seem to fit with our conclusions. Shore describes eight cognitive biases (Amos Tversky and Daniel Kahneman introduced the term

---

[1] *Source:* https://www.scientificamerican.com/article/do-video-games-inspire-violent-behavior/

"cognitive bias." Simply put, the term refers to the phenomenon where our brain simplifies new information based on what we already know. While in most cases this practice is useful and time saving, in many other cases it causes us to believe (and fiercely defend) faulty conclusions and specious arguments.) one of which he calls "causfusion." According to Shore, "causefusion" is a cognitive bias which causes us to attribute cause-and-effect to correlation.[2] A great example is the "causefusion" around eating ice cream and shark attacks. There is a strong correlation between eating ice cream and being attacked by sharks. So much so, in fact, that the more ice cream consumed, the greater the number of shark attacks. Isn't it reasonable to assume then that eating ice cream therefore must cause shark attacks? It may seem reasonable, but it is completely bunk. As with most "causefusion," there is one or more unknown elements at play and were we to know these elements, we would better understand the problem and address it far differently. In this case, people tend to eat more ice cream and go to the beach when it is hot outside, and hot temperatures also cause people to want to cool off, which increases the number of people both eating ice cream and swimming in the ocean. I know, it's not as cool as thinking that sharks wait patiently for the doughy blood-bags sticky with ice cream, but it's true. I think there is something more at play in our burning desire to blame violent video games, or violent movies, or the news media, or whatever, but the simplest answer is that some people are just fascinated with violence and enjoy hurting other people. This book won't focus on why. Instead, it will focus on ways to predict, prevent, and survive those rampage attacks.

Obsession With Violent Movies or Television Programs

Here again, it would appear to make sense that repeated and excessive exposure to violence portrayed in motion pictures and television programs would effectively train impressionable teens to become rampage killers, but again, psychological research does not

---

[2]*Source: https://www.amazon.com/Blunder-Smart-People-Make-Decisions/dp/1596916435*

support this conclusion. While it may be true that some rampage killers enjoy watching violent movies, there is growing evidence that the inverse is absolutely not true. This is like saying that fat people like brownies, so brownies—and brownies alone—cause obesity, and discounting or completely ignoring the many other contributing factors.When it comes to rampage killers—particularly adolescent rampage killers—it is easy to attribute cause when the cause seems self-evident But theories and conjecture that seem to make sense (without any empirical evidence) are the core of every urban legend. And after all, who doesn't like to take pot shots at young people? Even Socrates said, "Children; they have bad manners, contempt for authority; they show disrespect for elders and love chatter in place of exercise. They no longer rise when elders enter the room, they contradict their parents and tyrannize their teachers. Children are now tyrants." 2,492 years ago! But no matter how much people may WANT to blame the entertainment industry simply cannot be supported by actual facts; but why let facts screw up a good story?

Dog In The Chicken Coop

When I was a boy I lived on a farm. We raised chickens (more on that later) and each morning and evening my younger brother and I had chores related to the care and feeding of these filthy little bastards. One day our favorite family dog turned up missing. My mom in particular loved this dog. Dogs and cats on a farm are working animals, but this dog was more of a pet with a job. My mom worried when the dog didn't show up for her evening feeding and I was especially worried—dogs were often shot, hit by cars, caught in fox traps, or injured or killed in any number of ways.

The next morning the mystery was solved. When my brother and I went to do our chores we made a gruesome discovery that would have made Charles Manson giggle in delight. The coop was littered with feathers and blood. 30–40 chickens lay dead as our family dog crouched, head bowed in apparent shame. She knew she had screwed up BAD. My brother ran home to get my dad (the coop was on the ruins of my grandmother's farm about a ¼ mile up the road from our house.) I stood and coaxed my dog from underneath the roost, trying not to cry. In those days it was a foregone conclusion that the farmer would take any dog that engaged in this sort of activity out and shoot it. I was horrified that this dog that I loved had done this, and when my dad arrived at the scene I didn't bother to beg for my dog's life. It would do no good; the dye was cast.

My dad was angry to say the least (these chickens were a big source of our livelihood) but much to my surprise he wasn't angry at the dog ("that's just a dumb animal doing what it's instincts told it to do,") but at my brother and I. He called us halfwits, or damned dumb kids, or something equally affirming. He said that of course the dog would kill the chickens. The dog was locked in with them and they got scared. When they got scared, the dog got aggressive. The dog's aggression caused the chickens to panic and the dog's predatory instincts took control and she killed each chicken. As the chicken's panic intensified and the blood filled the dog's nostrils she killed more and more; her killing rampage ending only when all the chickens were dead.

Could it be that rampage attackers (who usually have a specific target in mind) are reacting, the way my dog did? Fueled by blood, carnage, and the rush of an apex predator killing its prey? No one can ever be certain—scarce few of the rampage killers survive, and those that do are unlikely to tell the truth if they even know what the truth is.

You don't hear much about bloodlust anymore, but maybe that is what these massacres are about—something buried deep in our primate medulla oblongatas that drives us to kill. Something that the sight of people panicked prey stimuli that the predator in the killer can't resist. Is it the scent of blood coursing through our nostrils the urges us on to battle like primitive warriors.

Or maybe it's simpler than all of that. Maybe they brought a big gun and brought a bunch of ammunition just in case they had to fight their way to their intended target, and then after the gunsmoke settled they used the ammo simply because they had it and they knew they were at the end of the road.

Death By Police

I interviewed people in law enforcement and asked them directly if they thought that rampage killers were trying to commit "death by police" (the act of forcing a first responder to kill you instead of taking your own life.) To a person, each dismissed the idea because, as one described the rampage killers, "They are cowards. They shoot up schools or their workplaces. They look for soft targets—you don't see many rampage attacks on police stations." Andrew Arena isn't so sure, " I am not sure suicide by cop is on the shooter's mind initially, but after it begins it may become a way to end the situation."

It's also worth mentioning that many rampage attackers aren't ultimately killed by police. So it these attacks are suicide attempts then they are doing it wrong. After they are out of ammunition, or it is obvious to them that they cannot possibly escape, some are arrested without further resistance.

Mentally Ill and Marginalized

When it comes to teens in particular,there seems to be an element of attention-seeking. If a teen can't be good academically, or athletically, or socially, he (these rampage killers are overwhelmingly male) can at least be notorious. Many have expressed the desire to have "the biggest body count ever" or the aspiration to be greater than whatever rampage killer happens to have impressed them. It is a way of screaming to the world, "I am someone! I will not be ignored!!" In the end we will probably never know what triggers these attacks to occur, but what we're doing now—restrictions on guns, increasing funding for school security et al, isn't working. We do know this: the teenage, and probably adult, rampage killers learn violence in the home, usually by watching domestic abuse. We are working on symptoms and not on the core problems of mental instability and domestic violence. Jonathan Gold adds a sobering thought, "It's a shame that we are in a place in our lives—in the twenty-first century—that this is our reality; where we have to prepare every day for the savagery of a stranger that commits this kind of act."

"And then the bullhorn crackles and the captain tackles with the problems of the hows and whys. And he can see no reasons, cause there are no reasons what reason do you need to die?"
—*"I Don't Like Mondays" Sir Bob Geldoff*

Stop. Don't Shoot!

Acknowledgments

This book would not be possible without the love and support of family and friends, my publisher and publicist, and most especially my daughter, who edited the word salad that comes out of my brain and dribbles down my arms across the keyboard and into the manuscript. When I began this journey of writing books for publication, my publisher insisted that no one else touch my words, lest they lose the voice of a madman swinging a bag of broken glass in a crowded room. My publisher felt that any editor would destroy my voice. There are misspellings in this book, unusual footnoting, and a host of other irregularities. All of these are mine. While my daughter did her best to convince me to take out a meandering, pointless anecdote, begged me to check the footnotes, and advised that I move some paragraphs or sections to other chapters I—after carefully considering each comment—decided to go with my ample gut and reject her suggestions.

I would be remiss to not mention the extraordinary help of Jonathan Gold, Giffords Senior Ambassador and President of Giffords Gun Owners for Michigan and Andrew Arena, retired FBI Division Chief, Head of Counter Terrorism, and expert in preventing workplace violence. And a thanks for nothing to all the heads of Human Resources who committed to contributing to this book but then left me hanging. (If you find this book helpful or useful please go into your company's Head of HR's office and spit on them.)

Of course—and I should have done this far sooner—I have to thank Colleen Kelly and Jeanne Murphy, whose infinite patience kept me plugging away when it was the last thing I felt like doing. I think I also need to send a much overdo shout out to Dr. Paul Marciano without his insistence (and perhaps blackmail) I never would have found a publisher or written a single book (never mind four).

Above all this book would not be possible without the sadistic lunatics who kill innocent people or the absolutely brain-dead dolts who commit mass shootings—inside and outside of the workplace; the National Rifle Association who defend gun ownership even in the face of mounting violence; the menagerie of maniacs that have crossed my path; and the sickening pus-bag bullies who made it so easy to understand how someone could go off the rails and shoot up a workplace.

As always there are people whose contributions have not been acknowledged here. All I can say is work harder and maybe (JUST maybe) I might mention you too.

Dedicated to the victims of gun violence, domestic violence, or other types of violence living and dead, and the loved ones left behind to pick up the shards of their shattered lives.

Contents

Stop. Don't Shoot!

Introduction

Years ago I was teaching a course on ethics and after class, one of the executives came up to me and shared an anecdote. "Last night when I got home, I was telling my wife about how funny something you said was," he began, "and my wife looked at me and said, 'did you go to a training course or a comedy club?' So then I told her about the concept that you were explaining and how I can apply that concept in my day-to-day work." Tben he looked at me with a very intense look on his face and asked me if I did that deliberately. I explained to him that I find that making a joke before or after making a serious point tends to help people retain the serious points. This book is about a serious issue. So serious, in fact, that were I not to lighten it up once and again it could become so depressing that I would struggle to write it and you would struggle to read it.

Parts of this book may be unsettling to some of you and difficult to talk about. But we can't settle for talking about it. We need to SCREAM about it. Nothing will stop until we drag its carcass out of the darkness and, as repellant as we may find it, act on it.

Stop. Don't Shoot!

Chapter 1: Background & History

Before we continue, I think it is important to dispel some dangerous information. This may be unsettling to some, but these are what grownups call "facts." Facts are based on what is known as "research," and much of it comes directly from the Bureau of Labor Statistics. So if you're going to bitch and whine about reality, tell it to someone else; I got enough idiots in my life as it is. It is important to clarify some very unsettling beliefs held by the ordinary people in our life; our friends, neighbors, and coworkers, and even strangers on the street.

Claim: Guns Don't Kill People, People Kill People.

Fact: No shit; neither do knives, nor baseball bats, nor staplers, nor toasters. Inanimate objects don't kill people, but guns in the hands of assholes DO kill people. Guns facilitate the killing of large groups of people. Guns are used to kill at range, rack up respectable body counts, and take out anyone who rushes to the victims' aid. Anyone who honestly believes that it's no harder to kill someone with a gun than it is with baseball bat or a knife is either a liar or too stupid to own a gun (or a knife or baseball bat.

Shit, if it were up to me they wouldn't be allowed to own a baseball HAT.)

Claim: The Second Amendment of the U.S. Constitution Gives Me The Right To Bear Arms.

Fact: True, but all rights have limits and corresponding responsibilities. Some will make the argument that they have a Constitutional RIGHT to own a gun—any gun up to and including a surface to air missile.[3] To them I say, you also have a right to remain silent, so why don't you try that for a change? America is unique in the fact that Americans are given the right to the pursuit of happiness. No other nation in the world (at least I'm told, and I'm too lazy to look it up) confers the right of its citizens to try to be happy. But just like gun ownership, the right to the pursuit of happiness has limits—just because you get your jollies sodomizing raccoons doesn't mean that this practice is a protected right under the U.S. Constitution.

Yes, the Supreme Court has ruled that the Second Amendment right to bear arms is an individual right, but in that same ruling it held that the right to form well-regulated militias was the right of the State, not the individual. So all you toy soldiers out there founding domestic terrorist groups are outlaws, and the actual militias (State Police, County Sheriffs, and local police departments) have the right to gun you down in your front yard. As John B. Finch said (and has been quoted by many more famous than him, hell, I think I am more famous than him,) "Your right to swing your arm leaves off where my right not to have my nose struck begins." He went on to say something that we are well advised to remember, "Here civil government comes in to prevent bloodshed, adjust rights, and settle disputes."

Andrew Arena, in addition to being a former head of Counter Terrorism for the FBI, unlike the mouthbreathers who purport to

---

[3] *yet*

know and understand the U.S. Constitution, holds a law degree and has this to say, "Under the Second Amendment we have the right to own guns; however, I believe strongly in "responsible" gun ownership. Too many people do the bare minimum to purchase/carry a handgun. You need to continuously train, to include "Shoot/Don't Shoot" simulators. More weapons in a location can definitely lead to additional issues if those in possession are not properly trained. There is also the issue of arriving law enforcement and armed people!"

Claim: All Rampage Attacks Are Mass Shootings.

Fact: It is true that there has been an uptick in rampage attacks where the perpetrator uses another weapon—knives, machetes, and even clubs—but the kinds of attacks that we will discuss in this book typically are mass shootings. As Jonathan Gold, Giffords Senior Ambassador and President of Giffords Gun Owners for Michigan, told me, "You can't kill someone with a machéte at 200 yards and you don't amass a huge body count with a knife." [4] Gold is an advocate for responsible gun ownership and an ex private detective who was the victim of gun violence before joining Giffords.

Claim: The Second Amendment of the U.S.Constitution Means the Government Cannot Take Away My Gun or Restrict Ownership In Any Way.

Fact: Rights are not entitlements. The U.S. Constitution was amended to include the Bill of Rights, not the Bill of Entitlements. So while you might have the right to own a gun, that right is not an unfettered entitlement, if it were, just as the Miranda rights guarantee that if you cannot afford an attorney one will be provided to you, the police would be offering you a handgun at no cost before they arrested you. As insane and absurd as that is, someone out there believes that this is the intent of the Constitution. With rights come responsibilities. In short, you may

---

[4] *Source: Conversation with John Gold*

have the right to bear arms, but that right ends at my right not to be a victim of gun violence; it ends at the schoolyard gate; and it ends at the workplace door. We have courts and peace officers who are here to settle your dispute. So bear your arms if you must, but recognize that you are responsible for every act of violence perpetrated using that gun, every crime committed with that gun, and every atrocity or terror caused by that gun. Just as I am culpable if my dog kills a neighbor's toddler, you must be accountable for however the gun you legally own is used, even if not by you.

Claim: I Have The Right To Defend Myself.

Fact: In some jurisdictions you do, in fact, have the right to "stand your ground" and even openly carry a firearm. But this right is fairly narrow. For example, I can't shoot my postal carrier because he or she is on my property. I also don't have the right to invite or lure someone onto my property for the purposes of killing them. Furthermore, I don't have the right to kill someone who is not attacking me, even if they are using threatening or aggressive language. Standing your ground becomes a homicide when you kill someone who isn't attacking. You also can't kill someone who is threatening to harm you but clearly does not have the means to carry out the threat. So for example, if you are driving by a pedestrian on the sidewalk and you hit a large puddle drenching him with muddy water and he shouts, "Come back here and I will kill you," you do not have the legal right to hang a U-turn and return to gun him down. Additionally these types of mass shootings would not be possible without the perpetrator first having hoarded weapons and ammunition or having easy access to both. No one needs a military grade weapon and 1,000 rounds of ammunition for home protection. Listen up people: the zombie apocalypse is not a real thing. And if you're worried about the collapse of civilization, take a lesson from the COVID-19 pandemic and hoard useful stuff like toilet paper, booze, and gasoline—anything that you can use as currency.

In other words, to the more studied among you, YOU DON'T HAVE THE RIGHT TO KILL SOMEONE WHO IS NOT ATTACKING YOU EVEN IF YOU'RE SCARED![5]

Claim: Workplace Violence is Decreasing.

Fact: While the number of workplace violence incidents has been steadily decreasing since 1994, this statistic is misleading. In fact, in his article "6 Things to Know about Mass Shootings in America: As We Mourn The Victims Of Another Mass Shooting, A Criminologist Takes On Misconceptions About Gun Violence" published in 2016 in *Scientific American,* Frederic Lemieux said, "A recent study published by the Harvard Injury Control Research Center shows that the frequency of mass shootings is increasing over time. The researchers measured the increase by calculating the time between the occurrence of mass shootings. According to the research, the days separating mass shooting occurrence went from on average 200 days during the period of 1983 to 2011 to 64 days since 2011.What is most alarming with mass shootings is the fact that this increasing trend is moving in the opposite direction of overall intentional homicide rates in the US, which decreased by almost 50% since 1993 and in Europe where intentional homicides decreased by 40% between 2003 and 2013."

[5]*Except in Wisconsin Apparently.*

So far, the number of mass shootings in the first half of 2021 was unprecedented, so much so that experts (if you want to know who, Google it) believe that gun violence is a type of contagion—people are killing each other because others are killing them.

Claim: Children who Grew Up Playing Violent Video Games, Listening to Violent Song Lyrics, or Watching Violence in Movies or Television Are More Likely to Become Violent Teenagers or Adults.

Fact: Research has found that like so many societal ills—bigotry, dishonesty, and aggressive behavior —children who exhibit violent actions learn that violence by observing this behavior in adults. Children are much more adept at differentiating between play/pretend violence and actual rage-induced violence than many people expect. Much as it is in the animal kingdom, the young engage in mock violence as a way of learning. Any parent who has tried to prohibit war toys and/or toy guns can tell you how their young child's imagination can change a hair brush into a pistol without any coaching.

Claim: Mass Shootings (or as I prefer to call them rampage attacks) are New.

Fact: The first recorded rampage attack (perpetrated using a firearm) was committed in what is now called the United States of America sometime in the 1760s.[6]

Claim: Violent Games Desensitize Children and Teens.

Fact: Many believe that violent children tend to be drawn to violent video games which appear to reinforce their already aggressive attitudes, but that becomes a "chicken or the egg" argument. Pedophiles tend to possess child pornography, but I don't know of any researcher who believes that child pornography *causes* pedophilia or the sexual abuse of a child. As it pertains to video games, according to Greg Toppono, author of "Do Video Games Inspire Violent Behavior? Conventional Wisdom Suggests

---

[6] *Conversations with former FBI Special Agent In Charge, Head of Counter Terrorism, Andrew Arena*

Violent Media Is Harming Kids. But Sometimes A Game Is Just A Game, ``"No one knows how any of these games—Dance Dance Revolution included—might have affected a kid who was clearly struggling. The truth is that decades of research have turned up no reliable causal link between playing violent video games and perpetrating actual violence. This is not to say that games have no effect. They're built to have an effect. It's just not necessarily the one that most people think."[7]

Claim: You are More Likely to be Murdered at Work Than Outside of Work.

Fact: The incidences of workplace homicides is much lower than homicides that take place elsewhere.

Clearly, this issue is important because 46% of workplace fatalities are homicides and they are, in fact, the leading cause of workplace deaths. And while workplace injuries have fallen over time, workplace fatalities continue to trend fairly flat. So while the problem may not seem nearly as bad as it was 25 years ago, for the many victims of workplace violence and those who mourn them, there is still a problem. And 25 years means that nearly an entire generation who understood the dangers of workplace violence have left the workplace and been replaced by workers who have little or no experience dealing with workplace homicides. To make matters worse, worker violence related to work but perpetrated outside of work is not calculated in these statistics. Instances where a lone gunman stalked workers and either shot and killed them as soon as they left the premises, or waited until they reached a nearby watering hole where he left them dead in the parking lot, don't get tallied[8] in the workplace homicide statistics. It's a problem, and my job in writing this book is to help you, in some small measure, to keep this from happening on your watch or to you. The outlook for continued spikes in workplace violence now that so many workers are working from home is fairly grim, and it is muddled by a situation that is not adequately addressed by the media,

---

[7] *https://www.scientificamerican.com/article/do-video-games-inspire-violent-behavior/#*

[8] *These statistics aren't considered workplace violence because the U.S. has a very narrow (and business friendly) definition of workplace violence, that is, a physical attack. Workplace violence is defined as a physical attack on a victim while in place of employment.*

researchers, or law enforcement. Jonathan Gold points out, "if there is a gun in the home it is far more likely that it will be used on someone in the home than it will be on an intruder."

The point is that no matter how logical we might find a correlation, we can't extrapolate from that data and conclude, for example, that because there are more women serving in the military (and therefore more comfortable with guns) that more women will commit gun violence against a co-worker; it is a belief unsupported by facts. So, let's stick to what we know to be true and leave the creation of urban legends to hysterical social media nitwits.

The bottom line is we believe these myths because they FEEL real. Common sense tells us that they MUST be true. We like having a nice, neat cause for rampage attacks because we love simple issues with simple answers. But before we outlaw video games, we should consider that while "90% of the children in the U.S. play violent video games"[9] an infinitesimally small number of these children grow up to be rampage killers.

In the past, perpetrators of rampage attacks tend to have had very specific, albeit twisted, motives and it was typically one of three: 1) a domestic squabble gone off the rails, 2) a real or imagined grievance against a group of people or 3) explosive anger at a boss or coworker. But the recent divisive politics, unregulated and unmonitored social media, and the isolation and politicization of the pandemic saw an increase in mental health issues, a startling growth in gun sales, and a frightening rise in domestic terrorism and hate groups.

It's also worth remembering that rampage attacks in the workplace may not seem to be the same as events at schools or other mass gatherings, but all of these settings are workplaces for SOMEONE. Schools have principals, teachers, administrative professionals, janitors, and so on; concerts or festivals have food vendors, performers, security and others, and while we may not see these as workplace violence events they most certainly are.

---

[9]*Source: Termpaperwarehouse.com*

Rampage attacks by unstable individuals tend to have at least one thing in common: attacking soft targets. Soft targets are targets that have little to no way of fighting back and with a few notable exceptions, most workplaces are soft targets. Soft targets offer several advantages to shooters: 1) soft targets pose no immediate threat, 2) soft targets offer the chance for the sick bastard to amass a large body count, and 3) soft targets are typically completely unprepared (or inadequately prepared) for an attack.

There are two types of rampage attackers: misguided glory-seekers, and gunmen with a specific target or targets in mind. The misguided glory-seekers want notoriety (for a long time I thought that meant someone who wanted to be a notary which was absolutely unimaginable to me. If you want to be a notary God bless you, but is it really worth killing for? As it turns out, notoriety is nothing of the sort.) There is a growing body of evidence that mass shootings are the result of the "contagion effect." Simply put, the "contagion effect"[10] is when an unstable person sees news reports of a mass shooting, the person will then become encouraged to perpetrate a mass shooting. Mass shooters often will espouse a hatred of this group or that, but the reality is that these asshats just like killing, as do serial killers. These individuals fit an altogether different psychological profile, and while this is certainly an issue worth discussing, here again, that is beyond the scope of this work.

The other type of rampage attacker has a specific target (or targets) in mind and may even attack a large crowd of people either out of frustration or to mask the initial motive for the crime. Both types of rampage attackers tend to have one thing in common: they have reached the end of their rope and don't see any way out except to go out in a blaze of glory.

So if there is a mass shooting, should we panic? Of course not, but we should do a better job of examining the safety and security measures of large gatherings of soft targets. I will address how to change a soft target into a hard target later in this book, but for

---

[10] *I forgot where I read this in all my research so just Google it.*

now, try to avoid large gatherings with lax or nonexistent security and where the population is particularly vulnerable.

Perpetrators of rampage attacks are people who feel that they have run out of options. Substance abuse, mental illness, an imagined or actual injustice by the employer, money problems, a lingering grudge against a coworker or a supervisor, or problems at home (remember 51% of mass killings begin with an intimate partner hoping to kill an estranged wife, girlfriend, or family member) or some combination thereof often set the workplace shooter into motion. In this work we will examine what elements tend to trigger these events. Imagine you have developed a drinking problem. Your drinking problem is expensive, but you can't miss more work, so you report for work unfit for duty because of a lack of sleep or a hangover, or you may even begin drinking on the job. You begin to use money that you earn to buy alcohol instead of paying the rent or mortgage, the utilities, and other household expenses and before long you have problems at work, problems with your spouse, and face losing your home, job, and family. A feeling of hopelessness sets in and there are some convenient scapegoats for all your problems: your wife, your boss, Human Resources, even co-workers that you suspect may have snitched on you. These people are all tangible targets (and potentially soft targets) and you have one last act of control in your life: the power to kill.

In other cases, things are far simpler: the shooter suspects his wife or girlfriend is cheating on him (rightfully or wrongly) and goes to the place he knows she (and potentially her illicit partner) will be: at work. This book will discuss more on this topic—predicting, preventing, surviving, and moving on—in later chapters. Of course working from home destroys the workplace as a sanctuary where one can feel secure, and this is an issue that will need to be addressed, and soon.

We believe these myths that rampage attacks are caused by exposure to violent movies, playing violent video games, and widespread media exposure because we WANT to believe these things; it helps us make sense of the motivation of a madman who guns down school children.

But There Is Hope

The purpose of this book is twofold: first, it is intended to aid you in screening applicants who might be at risk of perpetrating a single shooter event in the workplace, and secondly, this book will help you to spot individuals who are likely to be targeted for this type of attack, and by association put your workplace at risk. This book is important because employers have a moral, ethical, and legal responsibility for keeping their workers safe, and homicide is the leading cause of workplace death for women. At no point should this book or the information herein be used to illegally discriminate against women who might be targeted, but forewarned is forearmed and if you do knowingly hire a woman or man who is at high risk of being targeted you must take all necessary precautions to protect the individual and the company. Throughout this book I refer to the perpetrator as male; again, this is deliberate because women are at far greater risk of being murdered at work by a relative or a domestic partner and it is exponentially more likely that a man will be the killer.

The psychology behind this gender inequality is important, but frankly not as important as knowing that it is far more likely for female employees to be targeted than men. This statistic is somewhat misleading, as men tend to die in the workplace in greater numbers than women, and men are disproportionately more likely to be employed doing high-risk work. But the statistic that cannot be ignored is that across all industries, in the US at least, the incidence of death at the hands of a relative of a domestic partner is a scant 2% for men, and a staggering 42% (the single largest category) for a woman. This is an issue that has been ignored for too long, and I intend to address it with all the snarkiness and rancor that it deserves. For statistics to be this far out of whack means that companies aren't doing enough to protect women, either out of ignorance or incompetence. After reading this book you can no longer plead ignorance, but I can't do anything to make you more competent. You will either use this book as a wakeup call or remain living in a bubble and put people at risk.

Summary

Mass shooting and workplace violence essentially mean the same thing. Of course there are subtle, specific differences, but the more we know about the causes of the seemingly unrelated events, the more obvious it becomes that the triggers that set things in motion and the type of person who carries out these acts make the differences academic and of little practical use.

Thought Starters

How safe do you feel in your workplace? What would make you feel safer?

How would you account for the huge gender discrepancy between male and female victims?

How can companies be compelled to take action given these alarming statistics?

Workplace violence tends to be seen as a "non-problem" despite growing evidence that unless there is a fatality or hospitalization then incidences of workplace violence go unreported. How can we encourage open and honest dialogue about this issue?

What do the occupations that have the highest homicide rates (police officers, sales clerks, retail managers) have in common?

Stop. Don't Shoot!

Chapter 2: A Brief Overview of Gun Violence in America

W hen we talk about workplace violence, we could conceivably be talking about anything from a shoving match between two coworkers to a cold-blooded killer moving methodically through the workplace and killing all those he encounters. You might have noticed that I used the pronoun "he" in this sentence; that's deliberate. Perpetrators of workplace violence are disproportionately male and 85% of these crimes are committed using a firearm, although stabbings and beatings are not unheard of—victims just have a better chance of surviving these types of attacks.

The reality is this: guns allow one to kill from a much greater distance, amass a much greater body count, and kill from relative safety. I have been in a lot of bar brawls and schoolyard fist fights, and I tell my younger relatives and friends' children that it isn't about how much carnage you can inflict, it's about how much punishment you can stand there and take. Guns are a different story; it doesn't matter how big a milquetoast pansy you are, if you have a gun you can kill a single armed opponent without so much as seeing the whites of his or her eyes. So yeah, the problem isn't limited to guns, but even someone with a bow and arrow doesn't stand much of a chance against a military grade rifle.

We discussed the cognitive blind of causefusion (attributing cause and effect with correlation) so I won't drone on and on about how these are correlations and not cause and effect, and how drawing conclusions based on these correlations can be dangerous. There is a strong correlation between the age at which symptoms of autism typically manifest and the age at which children are vaccinated. So while a correlation does in fact exist, does this mean that cause and effect exists in these cases? Most doctors and researchers would give a resounding "no," and yet the belief still persists (largely promulgated by an ex Playboy centerfold who strongly believes that vaccinations caused her child's autism. But the blame doesn't rest there. The original study that linked vaccination to autism was retracted 12 years after its publication and its author was stripped of his medical license, but only after 12 years of social media warning parents not to vaccinate their children; the point being, the damage was already done.

Some other correlations worth considering are the number of women who are veterans of wars, the number of women suffering PTSD, etc. One could postulate that because the opportunities and life experiences of women now are dramatically different than they were in 1994, society would likely have seen an uptick in women committing homicides. Fortunately, no such uptick exists.

In *Gunman*, I wrote "...while gun rights advocates and opponents alike can argue over the extent of the problem, that is not the intent of this book." I was wrong. Guns are a problem, and while others can bury their heads in the sand when it comes to gun violence, I can't be silent anymore. For the record, I remain an adamant gun-ownership advocate, I just can't pretend that the majority of workplace violence is unrelated to guns. No one needs a semi-automatic rifle capable of killing a hundred people in minutes. Home protection? If you keep a gun in your home for protection, you are far more likely to kill yourself or a family member than an intruder. Furthermore, an intruder is far more likely to have his (it is overwhelmingly men) blood run cold at the sound of the telltale "schuck-schuck" sound of a pump shotgun putting a shell in the chamber than the sound of a dog, or of a person yelling "I have a gun" while aiming down the barrel of a Glock. I spoke with a lot of unsavory people while doing research for this book. One burglar who routinely invaded occupied dwellings told me that if he saw a woman with a handgun he would be tempted to rush her. His reasoning was that she was probably too shook up to even fire the gun. "But a shotgun," he told me, "it don't take no kind of courage to fire off a shotgun and that will fuck your shit UP!"

And even if you do kill an intruder, you then have to wait for the coroner and the cops to get done before you can clean up. Even if you think you can just vacuum around the dead intruder, you can't. After the hours it will take the cops to clear you and allow you to clean up have passed, those blood stains will never come out (as Lady Macbeth learned.) At first it will make a great conversation starter, but before long you will be lying about butchering hogs in your den. Your best bet is just to buy a nice throw rug.

The Difference Between a Mass Shooting and A Workplace Violence Event

The phenomena of mass murders is not a new or recent development. In the past we have had axe murderers, mad bombers, and an assortment of "rampage killers." Many used guns and many did not. Conventional wisdom tells us that when a nut in a tower shoots into a crowd of strangers and he has no particular target in mind, he is a mass shooter. But in reality, in most cases we don't really know what the motive for a killing was—even in cases where the killer survives. Oh sure, he may hate homosexuals, foreigners, blacks, Latinos, the government, the band Journey, or be following some twisted ideology, but most just want to kill a lot of people, any people. On Jan. 29, 1979 a 16-year old girl (I am not going to use these bastards' names and perpetuate their notoriety) sat in her house, picked up the .22 caliber rifle her father had purchased for her and lazily picked off three adults and eight children. A reporter was able to reach her by phone during her rampage and, when asked the question on everyone's mind—why—he simply responded, "I just don't like Mondays... I did this because it's a way to cheer up the day." Those cold-blooded words were immortalized by The Boomtown Rats in their biggest hit song "I Don't Like Mondays." People tend to like the explanation that the rampage killers don't have a specific target because it's comforting to think that something so horrendous could never happen to them.

Talking about the difference between a single shooter event (or a mass shooting) and a workplace violence event rapidly becomes an academic and banal conversation. It is almost impossible to differentiate between these events (remember parades, rallies, concerts—any mass gathering is usually staffed by someone, making it SOMEONE's workplace) because both are perpetrated in much the same manner, with only trivial differences. Whether it be attendees at a concert or a specific individual, there is very little productive or useful information that can be gleaned from why a person chose his or her target (we will talk about the types of circumstances that tend to trigger rampage attacks further on.) Most, if not all, of the events involve a specific target and in more than half the cases the target is an intimate partner or family member of the shooter. Sure, other people get killed, but they are just collateral damage. So we shouldn't be quick to dismiss a shooting as just some mad-dog killer acting at random. More often than not, the place, the victims, and the timing are carefully planned by the shooter.

Here are some grim statistics:

- **39,000 Americans die from gun violence every year—an average of 100 per day**. One has to be careful when using this argument with a gun nut because they typically respond with, "Yeah but how many people die in crashes a day?" This response to an argument is the person saying, "I don't have a counter to your very valid point so let me deflect by introducing my own unrelated point." I typically respond with, "Good point, and when we are discussing highway safety I will be glad to hear you out, but right now we are talking about gun violence."

- **97% of all gun violence is either from suicide or homicide, while only 1.4% is from police shootings and 1.3% is caused unitentionally.**[11] There is a common misperception that the police are on a killing rampage in the U.S., but this just isn't the case. I am a firm supporter of holding bad cops (and those who abet or cover up their crimes) legally accountable for police brutality, including and especially when this behavior ends in a fatality, but when it comes to gun deaths police-related gun civilian deaths are tiny compared to the gun deaths from other sources. The most alarming part of this statistic, for me, is that the smallest percentage of gun violence is unintentional. Most, by a wide margin, are the result of someone making a conscious decision to shoot themselves or someone else.

- **Nearly every American will know <u>at least</u> one victim of gun violence in their lifetime.**[12] Sadly, this doesn't surprise me. As I reflected on this particular point I did what you are perhaps doing now and started counting how many people I know who have been shot. I counted seven; all but one of them died, and only one of them was shot by a stranger.

---

[11]*Source: https://giffords.org/lawcenter/gun-violence-statistics/*

[12]*Source: https://www.everytown.org/issues/domestic-violence/*

- **Over 1 million Americans have been shot in the past decade and gun violence rates are rising across the country.**[13] Open carry and Stand Your Ground laws have emboldened people to shoot people, even those who in many cases were incapable of harming them. Take a look at your neighbors. Do you trust them not to put a bullet in your head because your dog took a crap on their lawn and you were bending over to collect the mess (hopefully with a bag and not your bare hands?)

- **In 2020, gun deaths reached their highest level in at least 40 years, with 39,773 deaths that year alone.**[14] This is an old statistic and doesn't consider the effect that the pandemic and lockdowns has had on homicides and suicides, but 2022 threatens to eclipse this number. There is a direct correlation between the proliferation of guns and gun deaths. The more guns and ammunition there are in the hands and homes of Americans, the more likely it is that these guns will be used.

- **Gun access triples suicide risk.** It stands to reason that if you are suicidal and have access to a gun, the probability is high that you will use that gun to kill yourself. More gun deaths are self-inflicted than caused by others, but what this statistic doesn't tell you is that in many cases it is not the gun owner who kills him/herself, rather it is a family member using someone else's gun.

- **The majority of suicides (51%) involve a gun.**[15] The purpose of our central nervous system is to keep us alive. The fight:flight response will shoot over 30 toxins into our bodies when we are exposed to danger, and these chemicals activate

---

[13] Source:https://www.everytown.org/issues/domestic-violence/#by-the-numbers

[14] Source: Sorenson, S. B., & Schut, R. A. "Nonfatal Gun Use in Intimate Partner Violence: A Systematic Review of the Literature". Trauma, Violence & Abuse. (2018). https://doi.org/10.1177/1524838016668589

[15] Source: Supplementary Homicide Reports, 1976-2019. Kaplan, Jacob concatenated files as posted on: Inter-university Consortium for Political and Social Research [distributor], 2021-01-16.https://doi.org/10.3886/E100699V10

every major anatomical system to jolt us into a reaction designed to save our lives. I don't want to sound judgmental, my intent is the opposite. My point is that not only is a self-inflicted gunshot wound the fastest way to kill oneself, it is also highly effective, much more so than other ways of killing oneself. It only takes a second to put a gun to your head and pull the trigger and while we don't know what was in the mind of the person in the moment before he or she decided to end his or her life, we do know that the greater the length of time that it takes to commit suicide the greater the chance that the person might change his or her mind and get help. Eliminating gun ownership won't stop suicide, but one should really consider this statistic before bringing a gun into their home.

- **Over half of women killed by an intimate partner are killed with a gun.**[12] I've gotten more than my fair share of grief by asserting that much of the workplace violence is an outgrowth of domestic violence. Even women's groups and feminist organizations don't want to talk about it (at least to me.) If there is a gun in the home (even if it is owned by the woman) there is far less time to escape the violence and a much higher chance of the result of the violence being a woman's death.

- **Every month, an average of 57 women are shot and killed by an intimate partner.**[13,14] I've made this point previously but it is important enough to mention it again. People often defend their purchase of guns by saying it is for "home protection," but the numbers don't lie—a gun in the home is more likely to be used to kill a loved one than to kill an intruder.

- **4.5 million women have reported being threatened with a gun by an intimate partner.**[3] For the life of me I can't understand why more people—both men and women—are startled by this statistic. Before people make a threat, they envision themselves carrying out the threat. I understand

41

the dynamic of domestic abuse, and I will not blame the victim. That having been said, long before the first punch is thrown there are numerous red flags and an intimate partner threatening to shoot you is a BIG red flag. You may love your intimate partner, but you can love them with a restraining order, you can't love them while lying in the morgue with a bullet in your head.

- **Access to a gun makes it five times more likely that a woman will die at the hands of a domestic abuser.**[3,15]

  o In more than half of mass shootings, the perpetrator shot an intimate partner or family member. [3]

  o Globally, domestic violence, or Intimate Partner Violence (IPV,) skyrocketed during the pandemic lockdown, but did not rise in the U.S. And in fact, in some cases it fell up to 50%—the consensus among IPV experts is that the cases most likely INCREASED, but the victims were unable to report the violence or get the resources they needed to report it. And while the incidences of domestic abuse has seemingly stabilized, the incidences of murder-suicide has increased dramatically. Even the statistic that IPV has fallen is misleading. While IPV has fallen almost 50% in some areas, it has spiked in other areas and as yet it is not clear why.[23]

- **Alcohol abuse is often a significant trigger in domestic abuse**. Alcohol abuse greatly increased during the pandemic. "Adults during COVID-19 reported high levels of alcohol consumption, with those who reported high levels of impact from COVID-19 reporting significantly more alcohol (both more days and total drinks) than participants who were not as impacted by COVID-19."[16]

---

[16]*Source:* https://www.ncbi.nlm.nih.gov/pmc/articles/PMC7763183/

- **Mass shootings in the US have increased nearly 73% over the same time period last year**[1]

- **Research shows violence spreads like contagion, so one incident increases the likelihood of another.**[26] This means that the more rampage attacks we have and the more widely publicized they are, the more likely we will have even more attacks; it's a vicious cycle and it will continue until something meaningful is done about it.

- **Researchers say little has been done to prevent the next mass shooting.**[27] I am not convinced of the veracity of this contention. While there may be little research on rampage attacks (my preferred nomenclature,) there has been plenty of research about the effects of things like violent television or movies and violent video games and the findings are worth repeating: VIOLENCE IS LEARNED IN THE HOME. I had difficulty finding any serious studies on the causes of child abuse and domestic violence and even fewer practical approaches to preventing domestic violence and child abuse. If we could somehow prevent violence in the home (or at least keep guns away from the fiends that perpetrate these crimes) we could eliminate up to 51% of all rampage attacks. Some wife/husband beater's Second Amendment's right doesn't include one's right to shoot up a school and kill children.

- **Rampampage attacks are virtually indistinguishable from workplace violence.** Almost ALL mass shootings are in SOMEONE's workplace, since most large gatherings of people have employees (security, vendors, service providers, etc.)[18]

---

[17] *Source:* https://www.insider.com/mass-shootings-increased-in-2021-gun-violence-experts-cite-contagion-effect2021-4

[18] *This is my own conclusion. If you disagree with it feel free to try and prove me wrong.*

Summary

The arguments and misconceptions around gun ownership have been around a long time, and even though the U.S. Supreme Court

ruled that the right to bear arms is an individual right (that is, the right of anyone in the United States) in the same ruling, it determined that the right to form "well-regulated" militias was a State right (so the belief that any group of yahoos can form vigilante organizations is NOT an individual right and only the States can organize militias.) Much of the rhetoric spread on social media has just recently become the subject of greater scrutiny and control.

Thought Starters

How does discussion of the Second Amendment and misinformation about the right to bear arms impact workplace violence?

How can you dispassionately discuss dangerous misperceptions about gun rights?

How can workplaces (private and public) restrict a person's right to bear arms without violating the Constitution of the United States (or similar documents around the world)?

Stop. Don't Shoot!

Chapter 3: Violence in Healthcare

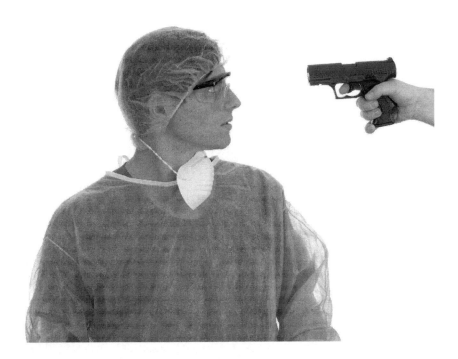

P erhaps the most difficult aspect of workplace violence is violence in the healthcare industry. I have been on both sides of this issue (although I never resorted to violence, I certainly can understand how one could.) Violence in the healthcare industry is a growing concern and very real problem. There are four main groups of people who can, and do, perpetrate violence in a healthcare setting: employees, visitors, intruders, and patients. For all involved, the healthcare environment is a stressful place to work, be a patient, or to visit.

What Triggers Violence in Healthcare?

While it is true that hospital workers live in a high-stress environment where there are days when everything is both urgent and an emergency, there are too many times where an overworked and stressed out hospital worker forgets that while their problems end at the end of a shift, the patient—and the patient's family—are stuck in hospital limbo. Cases that seem routine to a triage nurse or an intake clerk may be a primary stressor to a sick person or an injured person seeking immediate attention. For years hospital personnel have been taught (either formally or informally) to exert control, to always be in charge. Patients are routinely handed a clip board and told to fill out their forms before anyone even asks why they are coming into the hospital. Imagine being told to take a seat and wait until your name is called when you are worried that a loved one is on the brink of death and no one will listen to you when you tell them that your loved one needs to be seen NOW. Frustration builds and some people melt down and security is called. Maybe the irate person leaves, and sometimes that frustrated person returns with a gun. A gun says, "No, doctor, I am in charge!" And if this power is challenged, people often are injured or killed.

There is a key distinction between authority and power. Authority is the right to make decisions, conferred upon you by an organization, while power is the ability to make things happen. Some people, like police officers for example, have both power and authority. They have the authority conferred upon them by the population they serve, and the power that goes along with being armed with an array of weapons, both lethal and not.

Unlike so many other rampage attacks, rampage attacks in healthcare are often triggered by the way the rampage killer has been treated. In other words, simple active listening, empathy, and compassion can often de-escalate and prevent a rampage attack in healthcare.

Who is likely to perpetrate workplace violence in a healthcare setting?

Despite the pressures under which the employees work, employees are not the most likely demographic to commit a violent act in this particular workplace. As the following graph demonstrates, patients overwhelmingly are the most likely to act violently in healthcare settings.

Figure. Healthcare Worker Injuries Resulting in Days Away from Work, by Source

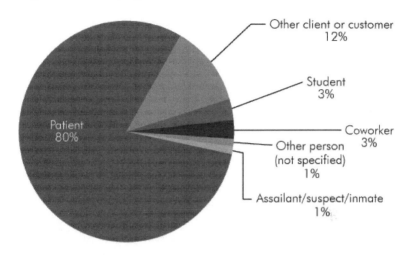

Source: Occupational Safety and Health Administration. Workplace violence in healthcare: understanding the challenge. 2015 Dec [cited 2017 Mar 29]. https://www.osha.gov/Publications/OSHA3826.pdf

MS17417

Eight out of every ten cases of workplace violence in healthcare are committed by patients, and an additional 12% are committed by other clients (sic) or customers (distraught family members, ex-patients angry about a bill, etc.) So 92% of all violence in healthcare is committed by patients and their families, while only 6% (if we consider students as coworkers; even though they are not seen as peers, they function in much the same ways as coworkers.) This leaves only 2% of the perpetrators of violence as individuals outside the facility's control (1% are criminals and the remaining 1% are what I can only assume are pharmaceutical reps hopped up on samples, behind on their quotas, and desperate.)

Another element that separates how society views violence in healthcare from violence in other settings is how violence is defined. When most of us think about violence, we are thinking about an aggressive action that causes physical harm to another person. But healthcare statistics include incidences like verbal harassment (from name calling to actual threats of violence,) sexual harassment (either a hostile work environment or quid pro quo, but not rape or sexually inappropriate touching.) I taught sexual harassment avoidance training for many years, and victims of sexual harassment can suffer tremendously from this behavior, but it does not rise to the level of rape, punches, and certainly not a mass shooting. This is a shortcoming of reporting violence in healthcare—in most industries, shouting at a coworker, while certainly inappropriate behavior, would not be considered "workplace violence." Until and unless we talk about violence using the same definition across all industries, and I am a strong advocate of defining it as an intentional act designed to physically harm another person or persons, studies like the one below are simply trivia.

In my book *Lone Gunman: Rewriting the Handbook On Workplace Violence Prevention*, I wrote; "According to a 2012 study conducted by Johns Hopkins, "almost 30% of U.S. hospital-based shootings occurred in emergency departments (EDs)..." Gabe Kelen, M.D, the lead author of the report, and the director of the Johns Hopkins Department of Emergency Medicine, said an in-depth review of the 154 hospital-based shootings, which resulted in 235 dead or injured, found that such shootings are difficult to prevent because most involved a "determined shooter." In my research for this book and for *Lone Gunman: Rewriting the Handbook On Workplace Violence Prevention* I did not find anyone involved in workplace violence who wasn't a determined attacker. Dr. Kelen also noted that "most perpetrators (of the shootings) had a personal association with victims," and "most of the events involved a determined shooter with a specific target." The study concluded that "common motives for shootings included a grudge or revenge seeking, and even euthanizing an ill relative." At the time when I wrote *Lone Gunman: Rewriting the Handbook On Workplace Violence Prevention* hospitals, despite the alarming rise in other forms of violence, did not experience a lot of rampage attacks, particularly shootings. Nonetheless, the findings verify many of the assertions I make in this book—the shooter is a determined attacker (often willing to take his own life) and that the rampage attacker usually has a personal relationship with the victim. Rampage attacks in healthcare facilities have escalated, and the FBI reports that there were 28 rampage attacks at healthcare facilities in 2019 alone. More recently, there were two rampage attacks (one in Tulsa, OK, and the other in Miami, FL,) which have sent the industry reeling. As recently as 2017, researchers were saying that rampage killer events were very rare in healthcare, (read; don't worry about it, it can't happen here.) Healthcare has finally come to realize that rampage attacks can occur at their locations, but I don't believe that they have yet come to realize that the likelihood of more attacks is rising because:

- **A Heightened Emotional State.** A slow day at a hospital still involves grouchy patients complaining just for the sake of complaining or visitors who make unreasonable demands because they are worried that their loved ones aren't getting sufficient care. Add to that medical professionals whose nerves are frazzled, an overcrowded and understaffed environment, and you have a virtual powder keg that can be ignited by the tiniest of sparks. But it doesn't stop there. Patients in pain grow irritable and desperate for relief and may have to be restrained. Med-seeking addicts may become agitated and violent when their efforts to gain drugs are thwarted. Visitors may become irate because they are dissatisfied with the care their loved ones are receiving. Someone who has tried to kill a patient may arrive at the facility intent on finishing the job. To many who work in healthcare, these are either everyday or infrequent occurrences, and these scenarios don't even consider the single shooter intent on finding a soft target. In fact, in many cases one of the leading causes of violence (as defined by healthcare) is nurse-on-nurse violence (although this is usually in the form of shouting or abusive language.) Even though healthcare facilities are seldom the setting of rampage killer events, it's easy to see how this environment could turn into a far uglier violent event than has previously been the case.

- **Lax/Inadequate Security.** I am old enough to remember when visiting a hospitalized patient meant checking in at a desk that was manned by an armed security officer (or at the very least there was an armed security officer conspicuously in the vicinity.) One would sign in upon entry (sometimes be required to produce identification) and out upon leaving. There was a limit of the number of people allowed in the patient's room at one time, and this limit was strictly enforced—both by the staff at the front desk and the nurses and orderlies. There were fixed visiting hours and little tolerance for people who did not abide by them. Now—and I've done this—one can show up and walk directly to a patient's room without being challenged.

When I worked as a consultant to a major healthcare system, I would routinely walk the halls and enter areas where visitors usually weren't present. I wore no badge identifying myself as a contractor, and yet was allowed to walk through areas where drugs were stored and any manner of potentially deadly instruments and tools lay unattended. Never once in the year as a consultant to this facility was I ever challenged about why I was there or who I was there to see. And if I was a security threat, the response time of the security department (through no fault of its own) was incredibly slow for a situation where every second could literally mean the difference between life and death. Once on the scene, the responding security officers often had to ascertain exactly why they were called and the precise threat—it could be everything from a violent patient to a stolen baby to an armed intruder. When it comes to security threats, there is no such thing as a "typical" security call. And if any security force should be prepared to shoot a violent person it should be a hospital security guard—they can treat the injured attacker on the premises.

Inadequate security measures are not necessarily the fault of the individual. In recent decades, patient satisfaction and the patient experience have become important measurements in healthcare. How important is it? According to an article on Guidewaycare's blog:

"Regulatory agencies increasingly seek to link patient experience scores to reimbursement. There is still some disagreement, however, over whether these scores can be neatly linked to outcomes. Ultimately, though, the consensus seems to be growing that experience of care does play a role in quality, and devoting resources towards improving patient experience, and ultimately satisfaction, provides value for both the patient and the hospital."

Having worked in healthcare, I can tell you firsthand of the intense importance healthcare providers place on the results of patient and experience surveys. As the quote indicates, there is intense pressure placed on providers to lower costs and poor performances. These areas are often used to justify cost reduction penalties. Unfortunately, none of the nine categories on the Hospital Consumer Assessment of Healthcare Providers and Systems (HCAHPS) survey address patient or worker safety or the overall security of the facility. I have written many published articles and have spoken several times on the fact that organizations tend to see improvement in the areas where they measure performance, and the fact that there is little incentive to perform in areas that are not measured. This makes healthcare facilities the next killing fields for unstable single shooters. I am not saying that healthcare facilities didn't need to improve their interaction with patients and families, however, I think the pendulum has swung too far. There is a way—my experience working for a healthcare system has shown me—to ensure the safety of workers, patients, and visitors without making anyone involved feel as if they are imprisoned.

- **Incongruent Expectations**. For healthcare workers, being overworked and under-staffed is just another day at the office. The hours are long as well as emotionally and physically demanding. There is often too much work to do and too few hands with which to do it. I have many friends and relatives in the healthcare profession (the by-product of working in the field,) and without exception they care so much about their patients. It is sad and embarrassing how misaligned their compensation is to the amount of dedication they show for the job. This is not to say that medical professionals can't be disgruntled, snotty, or outright rude, but that is beside the point. The life-and-death, break-neck urgency and nonstop pressure of the work environment can create a misalignment between the patient's or visitor's expectations and the actual care received. The nurses expect the patient and visitors to show a modicum of gratitude for all the things the staff are doing for the patient, and the patients and visitors expect the nurses to drop everything to respond to a call button (bear in mind the patients are typically heavily monitored with a number of devices, which allows the staff to sort out a life-threatening condition from a comfort request such as another pillow, a glass of water, etc.) The staff expect and deserve more than a little patience, but the patients and visitors don't really care that there was something more urgent—they are paying a lot for treatment and they expect to be treated well. Incongruency in expectations extends beyond healthcare personnel and patients of visitors. Oftentimes the perspectives of doctors differ distinctly from those of nurses, and the perspectives of clinicians can differ dramatically from the perspectives of support staff and administrators. Conflicting expectations create a lot of chaos and discord, and chaos and discord can create a toxic environment.

- **Soft Targets.** One of the unintended outcomes of the push toward improved patient satisfaction and the patient experience is a lessening of the importance of following the rules of facilities. And in the case of soft targets, one of the most important rules is to have visitors check in before heading to the patient's room. The purpose of having people check-in at a healthcare facility is primarily for the facility to know who is in the building and where they are in case an emergency evacuation is required. Ignoring this rule potentially allows a rampage attacker to proceed unchallenged to who knows where. Rules exist for a variety of reasons, but chiefly rules exist, in the most broad sense, to protect us by making behaviors predictable. Visiting hours are in place so that the hospital staff can quickly identify the people who are supposed to be in the hospital at the allotted times. Similarly, badges and key cards that must contain the wearer's photograph serve a similar purpose while adding the additional protection of restricting the wearer's access to only approved areas.. We will explore soft targets and how you can transform your workplace from a soft target in later chapters.

- **Criminal Behavior.** When we think about criminal behavior in hospitals or other healthcare settings, our minds inevitably turn to drug-related crimes—drug seeking addicts, theft of drugs by employees, etc. While crimes involving drugs is certainly a problem in healthcare, violence—from verbal and physical assaults to rampage attacks are now a reality.

- **Unstable Individuals**. People receiving care and the people who love them, who may otherwise be stable, productive, and law-abiding individuals, can be driven to violence because of stress, drug interactions, psychotic breaks, and more. Many normally well-adjusted individuals with no history of mental illness can actually become unstable in a healthcare setting. My late father, for instance, is an excellent example. While in the hospital for treatment, he was given morphine, a drug that—to the best of my knowledge—he had never received prior to this visit. While under the influence of morphine, he became convinced that the hospital staff was conspiring to harvest his organs. He got out of bed, hid behind a door, and attacked two nurses when they entered, punching one and pushing the other aside before he ran and hid. My sisters arrived to visit shortly thereafter only to find my father restrained to his bed. He snarled at them and called them "a bunch of crooks," all the while insisting that they too were part of the conspiracy. My father had no history of violence, and prior and subsequent to this event had never assaulted anyone. Was this outbreak foreseeable? Yes, as this was the first time the patient had ever been given morphine and this type of reaction has been well documented. It is reasonable to assume that the hospital staff would have taken precautions before giving the patient morphine, but they did not. What makes matters worse is that this same type of situation happened AGAIN! Even though my father and my sisters warned the staff about the issue. Fortunately, no one was seriously injured in either case.

Summary

Healthcare workers literally make life-and-death decisions every day. What's more, these life-and-death decisions aren't limited to patient care. Psychotic patients, desperate drug-seeking individuals who wander into the workplace unchallenged, worried family members—emotionally overwrought with worry and anxiety over the care of a loved one--and of course, all of the other antecedents to violence that we will explore in this book, can lead to the need for split-second decision making as well. Above any other workplace, healthcare stands alone as a hotbed for violence. The sheer level of violence in healthcare is frightening and the normalization of workplace violence, especially within healthcare, is terrifying. All of this was true BEFORE the COVID-19 pandemic that made the situation far worse in healthcare, and it is genuinely unclear how the pandemic will change statistics moving forward. We may not know for decades the extent to which the pandemic has impacted workplace violence in healthcare.

Thought Starters

Does defining violence in healthcare differently (including assaults between employees and abusive language as violence) than in other locations increase or decrease the chances that single shooter events will occur? Is this dangerous? Why or why not?

Since 92% of the perpetrators of workplace violence in healthcare fall under the direct control of hospitals (where the percentage is much lower in other industries,) should workplace violence be addressed differently in healthcare than it is in other settings? How should it be addressed?

How dangerous is it for healthcare providers to define violence in a different way than other industries? Why or why not?

How can healthcare administrators balance the demands of the patient experience with protecting workers, patients, and visitors?

Stop. Don't Shoot!

Chapter 4: Rampage Attacks

on Schools

First and foremost in many people's minds is the sickening number of rampage attacks on schools and that is completely understandable to me. When *Lone Gunman: Rewriting the Handbook On Workplace Violence Prevention* was published in 2019 the latest statistics on school shootings were at least five years old. It appears that cloistered monks can copy the Bible faster than government agencies can compile statistics. In fact, when I wrote the book I didn't touch on attacks on school shootings because, despite making for good emotional news stories, there wasn't much of a public outcry. That is a necessary change we needed to make.

According to Education Week's website, "There have been 40 school shootings this year that resulted in injuries or deaths, the most in a single year since Education Week began tracking such incidents in 2018. There have been 132 such shootings since 2018. Prior to 2022, the highest number of school shootings with injuries

or deaths was last year when there were 34. There were 10 in 2020, and 24 each in <u>2019</u> and <u>2018</u>."[19]

Parallels

I am shocked and sickened by the frequency with which I hear another report of a school shooting, but this book is not about my feelings (which is just as well because I'm really crabby right now.) There are both some strong parallels and important differences between attacks on schools and hospitals:

- Both hospitals and schools are soft targets chock full of highly vulnerable targets. Hospitals have bedridden patients and schools have children who are probably unlikely to possess the strength to fight back.

- Hospitals and schools are quasi-public facilities. Both have frequent visitors (although events like school assemblies, music recitals, and plays are not everyday occurrences, they do occur often and become part of the normal operation of a school.)

- Both are accustomed to strangers coming into the building.[20]

- An attacker has likely been in the building before (as a visitor or a student/patient.)

Differences

- A school's reaction plan is widely known and publicized in the media.

- A rampage attack in a healthcare facility is typically focused on a single individual and anyone who tries to stop him, while a similar attack at a school is usually committed

---

[19]*Source: <u>https://www.edweek.org/leadership/school-shootings-this-year-how-many-and-where/2022/01</u>*

[20]*My high school had a strict policy of having the door locked at all times, but all I needed to do was say my name through the intercom and say I was dropping off my fictional son's lunch and I would be in the building and have enough time to kill everyone in the office. Note: my principal was a great guy and died tragically young so don't call the police.*

by a teen or someone in his early twenties who may not have a grudge against the specific school at all.

- An attack on a hospital is typically in response to an actual or perceived grievance; the attacker—rightfully or wrongly—sees himself or a loved one as having been wronged, while attacks on schools seem to be based on a desire to be notorious.

- Healthcare attackers don't seem to try to amass a record setting body count, school shooters do.

You're Doing it Wrong

I will address the limitations of the "run, hide, fight back" model later, but in my opinion not only is this model dated, it is particularly dangerous in a school shooting. Personally, I would pull the fire alarm. Kids and teachers drill for that, they head (in an orderly fashion) to the nearest exit as the screaming sirens of ambulances, fire trucks, rescue vehicles, and police cars converge on the scene. All the while, the blaring of the fire alarm makes it difficult for the attacker to think—this was not likely part of his plan. The ensuing chaos may actually cause the attacker to flee. Once you are clear of the crime scene, call 911 and alert them of the attack.

In writing this book I spent countless hours researching the topic and as I did I discovered that a lot of self-appointed experts out there are spreading a lot of downright dangerous information that in my opinion was more likely to get someone killed then it was to save a single life. As someone who is viewed by many as a true expert, Andrew Arena said, "We have seen an unbelievable increase in so called "experts" in this field. I have a saying I begin my presentations with; If someone says they are an expert, they are either a liar or a fool! Get away as soon as possible. I believe there are people and companies who have experience. I completed the training given by the FBI and was also involved in MANY critical incidents. They key is I MADE A LOT OF MISTAKES! I tell potential clients that they need to look at the background of the "experts" they are engaging. What is their experience, training, etc.? This industry, like terrorism post 9-11, has become a cottage industry. Opportunities abound to make money. Make sure you are not hiring an imposter!"

One can argue that students all leaving the classrooms at the same time makes it easier to amass a large death toll, but I disagree. School children drill for fires so frequently that it is a far better strategy than the current model which should be called "cluster the targets" which is like shooting fish in a barrel for the attacker.

One can also argue that schools already drill for mass shootings, but Jonathan Gold is adamantly against these drills, "In my mind, having children drill for a mass shooting is child abuse." I agree with Jonathan Gold. I don't believe it is good for children to be continually reminded that there is an infinitesimal chance that they and their friends and teachers might be killed and have them drill for it. I think it contributes to chronic unease and anxiety disorders. I grew up with my parents telling me not to ride with strangers, not to talk to strangers, and not to take candy from strangers. I became a weird and worried child who obsessed over the chance that I would be kidnapped.[21]

Summary

Despite the best intentions of educators, schools remain a soft target, and what's more the number and frequency of rampage attacks are increasing. On one hand we want our children to be prepared. On the other hand, too much preparation can lead to chronic unease and mental illness. What's more alarming is that schools not only follow a reaction model that doesn't work, they also broadcast it so frequently that virtually any rampage attacker knows exactly how the target will react.

---

[21] *This was exacerbated as there was an active serial killer, The Oakland County Child Slayer, who preyed on children at that time operating not far from my home. The killing stopped but the crime remains unsolved. I didn't do it and have airtight alibis. Besides, I am too lazy to be a serial killer and was never a boy scout. As near as I can tell no known serial killers were boy scouts, but between learning to navigate in the woods, dig holes, light fires, and track prey, it's pretty good training for a serial killer. They even give you a really cool knife and a hatchet for crying out*

Thought Starters

Do you agree that the existing model of clustering children in small, enclosed spaces is a misguided model? Why or why not?

Many of the rampage killers that target schools are disenfranchised, isolated loners that likely had a rough time in school. How can schools address this population so its members don't grow up to be rampage killers?

Stop. Don't Shoot!

Chapter 5: Gun Violence in the Home Workplace

This is an extremely difficult chapter to write, perhaps not for the reasons you suspect. I learned the hard way that people don't want to talk about injuries, but even more they don't want to think about violence. People cringe if I bring up workplace violence or quickly change the subject if I talk about the connection between workplace violence and domestic abuse. Weirdly, they seem to be strangely serene in conversations about mass shootings (perhaps because that is something that happens to other people; people they don't know.) Well, it's time to grow the fuck up. People are dying and we can stop it. Not with words, or reading books, or clucking our tongues (except for the tongue clucking, these are great ways to prepare,) but we have to grab this beast by the horns and wrestle it to the ground.

But there are barriers to face, large barriers that can easily make the task seem insurmountable—a lost cause.

What is working from home? To answer that, we need a legal definition of a "worker," "work," and a "home workplace." When does our home become our workplace? What protections do we have in our home office? What OSHA regulations are in place to protect us when we are "working from home?" We have to rewrite a lot of definitions that have existed for a century or more, and that is an ongoing process. But violence won't wait, so we can't wait. In the interim we will just have to treat the home workplace as we would the traditional office workplace.

The pandemic drove many people from their offices to working from home, and while many people loved having virtual meetings and working in their pajamas, for others it became a deadly nightmare from which there was no escape.

This is uncharted territory for most employers. For many companies the choice during the pandemic was either allow (or require) individuals to work from home or shutter their companies until the pandemic was pronounced over. Companies long resisted the idea of employees working from home, more out of a misguided (at least in my experience) belief that if employees were allowed to work from home they would lollygag around, watch TV, run errands, and generally act like the lazy buffoons that all employees are in the eyes of most employers. And now workers have found that by not having a morning and evening commute, eating lunch out more than they should, and having their productivity sapped by inane conversations about bagels in the breakroom, they have far more time to focus on their actual jobs and be more productive. Consequently, employers are finding that they benefit from a remote workforce, but some of these advantages have disturbing implications.

The Employer's Obligation Within The Home-Work Environment

As it turns out, the Occupational Safety and Health Act (OSHA) has addressed the topic of work-at-home employees. Unfortunately, OSHA did not foresee the rapid and widespread movement from offices and field work and the massive rise in the number of people who work from home offices. Several decades ago, the tax code was changed such that home offices were no longer tax deductible, which I add here just to demonstrate how painfully out of touch the federal government is with the realities of today's workforce. The following excerpt from an OSHA website does a satisfactory job of explaining the current view of an employer's duty to protect work-from-home workers from injuries, illnesses, and attacks. This excerpt says it better than I can so I will lazily quote it here instead of paraphrasing it.

"The OSH Act applies to work performed by an employee in any workplace within the United States, including a workplace located in the employee's home. All employers, including those which have entered into "work at home" agreements with employees, are responsible for complying with the OSH Act and with safety and health standards.

Even when the workplace is in a designated area in an employee's home, the employer retains some degree of control over the conditions of the "work at home" agreement. An important factor in the development of these arrangements is to ensure that employees are not exposed to reasonably foreseeable hazards created by their at-home employment. Ensuring safe and healthful working conditions for the employee should be a precondition for any home-based work assignments. Employers should exercise reasonable diligence to identify in advance the possible hazards associated with particular home work assignments, and should provide the necessary protection through training, personal protective equipment, or other controls appropriate to reduce or eliminate the hazard. In some circumstances the exercise of reasonable diligence may necessitate an on-site examination of the working environment by the employer. Employers must take steps to reduce or eliminate any work-related safety or health problems they become aware of through on-site visits or other means.

Certainly, where the employer provides work materials for use in the employee's home, the employer should ensure that employer-provided tools or supplies pose no hazard under reasonably foreseeable conditions of storage or use by employees. An employer must also take appropriate steps when the employer knows or has reason to know that employee-provided tools or supplies could create a safety or health risk."

Okay, so it isn't exactly Shakespeare, but it is a nice synopsis of what the law says. So let's take a look at what this means to us in today's context.

> The OSH Act applies to work performed by an employee in any workplace within the United States, including a workplace located in the employee's home. All employers, including those which have entered into "work at home" agreements with employees, are responsible for complying with the OSH Act and with safety and health standards.

This is pretty straight forward. It says that any employer covered by the OSHA regulations has to follow these regulations irrespective of where the employee is working. "All employers, including those which have entered into 'work at home' agreements with employees..." Simple, right? Not exactly. Let's look at the phrase, "All employers, including those which have entered into 'work at home' agreements with employees..." First, "all employers" doesn't really mean *all* employees, according to:

https://www.osha.gov/sites/default/files/publications/all_about_OSHA.pdf,

"Not Covered under the OSH Act (include):

- The self-employed;
- Immediate family members of farm employers; and
- Workplace hazards regulated by another federal agency (for example, the Mine Safety and Health Administration, the Department of Energy, or the Coast Guard.)"

At first glance the number of employees covered by OSHA regulations seem pretty exhaustive, but on close inspection there are some dangerous loopholes:

The Self-Employed

I have interviewed hundreds of executives and business leaders who extolled the virtues of "the gig economy." The term "gig economy" is just a nice way of saying that a company will only employ you when they need you. On the surface this makes sense—how many of us have a plumber on retainer, or pay a mechanic 40 hours a week (plus benefits) because something might go wrong with our cars? But there is a darker side of this jubilant enthusiasm for the gig economy. In real terms it means:

- **Paying Double Taxes.** When you are self employed you are paying both the employer's portion of payroll taxes and the employee portion.

- **Much Higher Insurance Taxes**. I spent four years as a self employed consultant (I loathe that term, I would rather be called a pedophile than a consultant—for me it conjures up the vision of a sleazy car salesman in a ill-fitting polyester suit with an onion for a head and leeches for lips. When I first worked as a consultant I was told that the primary job of a consultant is to find his or her next consulting gig,) and I still refer to this time as when I worked for the Devil. The salary was attractive, that is, until I discovered that I needed a full-time bookkeeper, a tax attorney, could only afford catastrophic health insurance, and essentially the cost of being my own boss was exorbitant.

- **If You Don't Sell, You Don't Eat.** When I left my first consultant gig and took traditional employment with a small business I took an almost 20% pay cut, but still found myself with more cash than I was making in my days working for the Prince of Darkness. I had decent (but not great) insurance and job stability. When I was producing a video I enlisted the services of a company that was formed by several former colleagues. When I looked at their price, I was shocked! It was about 40% below what I was expecting and it made me worry a bit about their ability to deliver. When I expressed these concerns, they explained that working for yourself was like hunting a bear. You track the bear, you kill the bear, you drag the bear back home, and you skin the bear (personally I would have skinned it in the wild so I would have less to drag home, but that is not germane to our example.) They told me that was essentially the extent of their work. Unfortunately, while they were all out doing that, they weren't tracking the next bear and so they would see lengthy gaps in their income stream. They were more than willing to cut me a special rate because I was essentially tracking the bear for them by feeding them video production after video production. But even in this sweetheart deal there would be times when I didn't need a video crew and therefore had not "bear" to feed them.

- **Become Sick Or Injured As A Direct Cause of the Work You Do? Tough.** Because of the way we structure Workers' Compensation "gig workers" have literally no legal protection under OSHA and unfortunately, you won't know how valuable that is unless something very bad has happened to you.

What's worse is that many unscrupulous employers are pushing workers into these "side hustles" or self-employment, to make greater profits and avoid key protections for workers under the law.

Immediate Family Members of Farm Employers

I grew up on a farm and I am with Henry Ford who said "farm work is a life of drudgery." And like Henry Ford, I left farm life behind me decades ago. But when OSHA was conceived, they weren't envisioning farms as billion dollar global conglomerates, and even if they WERE envisioning them as such, it makes no sense that the son of a farmer who is employed as the business accountant is not entitled to worker safety protections. Of course agricultural work is seldom done at home—I can't remember the last time I slaughtered a steer in my basement—but wait...this is why we need a definition of the word "home." If one is an immediate family member of a farm employer, it is not beyond the scope of reasonableness that "home" might be a 100 acre farm. So whether you're bailing hay, or gathering eggs, or butchering hogs, or doing the payroll, does it make sense that you don't have any protection from OSHA regulations?

Workplace Hazards Regulated By Another Federal Agency

This exclusion may seem fairly innocuous, however, unlike OSHA provisions that allow individual states to enact worker safety and health legislation provided the state legislation is as or more stringent than the federal OSHA requirements, no such qualification exists in this portion of the OSHA requirements. So while one might assume that other federal agencies may have worker protections more stringent than OSHA, that may not be the case, and that means that requirements for worker protections against a rampage attack may not exist.

Even when the workplace is in a designated area in an employee's home, the employer retains some degree of control over the conditions of the "work at home" agreement. An important factor in the development of these arrangements is to ensure that employees are not exposed to reasonably foreseeable hazards created by their at-home employment.

Essentially, this says that your employer has certain rights to enforce safety procedures even if your workplace is in your home. Unfortunately, this statement by OSHA presupposes that the worker and company HAVE a "work-at-home agreement" and that there is some common, legal understanding of exactly what that document is. For all intents and purposes, there is currently no such thing as the "work-at-home agreement." Without a "work-at-home agreement," a worker has no protection and the employer has no legal requirement to protect a worker who is working from home. This never used to be a big deal until the pandemic turned the definition of working on its ear. Trust me, this is going to be a much larger problem as more and more workers eschew the traditional workplace model and more and more employers insist on the traditional workplace.

Employer Responsibility for Work-At-Home Workers

According to OSHA, "An employer is responsible for ensuring that its employees have a safe and healthful workplace, not a safe and healthful home. The employer is responsible only for preventing or correcting hazards to which employees may be exposed in the course of their work. For example: if work is performed in the basement space of a residence and the stairs leading to the space are unsafe, the employer could be liable if the employer knows or reasonably should have known of the dangerous condition." Am I the only one who finds this absurd? How could my employer, who is a 5 hour plane ride from my home, ascertain where in my home my workplace is, and furthermore whether or not there are hazards within my home? Add to the confusing language already on the books in OSHA regulations the fact that workplaces—even and perhaps more so—in a home office are so poorly defined and you have the miasmic mess that is the OSHA take on "work-from-home" safety.

The OSHA website is quick to point out that "There is no general requirement in OSHA's standards or regulations that employers routinely conduct safety inspections of all work locations. However, certain specific standards require periodic inspection of specific kinds of equipment and work operations, such as:

- ladders (§1910.25(d)(1)(x)) and §1910.26(c)(2)(vi));

- compressed gas cylinders (§1910.101(a));

- electrical protective equipment (§1910.137(b)(2)(ii));

- mechanical power-transmission equipment (§1910.219(p));

- resistance welding (§1910.255(e)); and

- portable electric equipment (§1910.334(a)(2)).

Although some of these operations may not be found in home-based workplaces, nevertheless, if an employer of home-based employees is aware of safety or health hazards, or has reason to be aware of such hazards, the OSH Act requires the employer to pursue all feasible steps to protect its employees; one obvious and effective means of ensuring employee safety would be periodic safety checks of employee working spaces.

This letter addresses only the employer's responsibilities under the OSH Act. Depending on what kind of business the "at home" employer is engaged in, he or she may have additional responsibilities under other federal labor or environmental laws, as well as under state laws of general applicability, such as public health, licensing, zoning, fire and building codes, and other matters." So rather than clarify the issue, OSHA once again obfuscates the issues. What is clear is this:

- Employers are responsible for providing a workplace that is free of foreseeable hazards.

- OSHA is hiding behind the Fourth Amendment to get out of investigating personal homes for safety violations.

- The involvement of employees is key:

  o to ensuring the fullest protection of employees in the workplace;

  o to properly identifying and assessing the nature and extent of hazards; and

  o in determining the effectiveness of the employer's efforts to establish and maintain a workplace safety and management program.

Employees can refuse to cooperate with all of the above.

If you work from home and you think OSHA will protect you from injuries, you are delusional. And if you think OSHA will force your employer to protect you from a workplace violence incident in your home, you are tragically and dangerously mistaken. Sadly, there is nothing the at-home workers can do, shy of joining a

Union, and even then there are so many poorly defined elements and loopholes that even a labor agreement would be tough to craft to address these shortcomings.

Corporate Responsibility: The Moral Argument

The question as to whether or not a corporation has a moral imperative to protect workers from violence when the workers are working-from-home is a bit like asking if the scorpion has a moral obligation not to sting the frog as it crosses the river. Of course it does. And even though the scorpion tries to justify administering the lethal sting by saying "it's my nature," it does not condone the behavior any more than executives arguing that some despicable act they have committed is in the best interests of the organization. From not butchering the neighbor's dachshund to policing up your dog's mess, we are all confronted with moral imperatives on an on-going basis. Some of us do them and a lot of us...well a lot of us have to keep our dachshunds under constant surveillance.

The U.S. Supreme Court has ruled that corporations are people, and as such, afforded the same protections as an actual person under the law, with some limitations. Arguing that corporations have a legal or moral obligation to protect workers can quickly devolve into a semantic and pointless argument. Many employers would rather give out grief wreaths than extend a helping hand. This book—in the following chapters—will forever nullify the argument that "there was no way of knowing and there was nothing I could do," so read the rest of the book with caution.

Protecting Workers Despite Having No Regulatory Responsibility To Do So

I mentioned in *Lone Gunman: Rewriting the Handbook On Workplace Violence Prevention* that one of my former employers had two cases—less than a month apart—of workplace violence. One junior executive made the mistake of saying that these cases didn't count because neither happened on the company property. The CEO responded in a rage with "I don't care WHERE this happened! These were our people and it doesn't matter to me if they were killed on our property, in our parking lot, or off property; they matter! EVERYONE COUNTS!" I met with him the next day and he told me point blank that I was going to become an expert on workplace violence prevention, and so began my journey into this sordid and disturbing world.

In both cases, a jealous estranged husband shot and killed his wife who was divorcing him. In one case, he waited just down the road from our factory exit, followed her as she left work, drove up next to her, and shot her dead. He was quickly apprehended by police, but it was small comfort to those of us who knew her. In the second incident, an estranged wife and a male friend were leaving work to head to the local watering hole to meet a large group of co-workers for an after work drink. When the two got out of the car in the bar parking lot, the estranged husband shot and killed them both. People speculated as to why the man who accompanied her was also killed, but no one will ever know for sure; and really, what difference does it make?

Not all workplace violence ends in tragedy. In still another case at the same company, one woman reported that she was divorcing her husband and that he had threatened to kill her. The Human Resources department respected her privacy, until a short time later when the man came into the parking lot and was stopped at the door by one of the workers. The Human Resources Manager, an executive who was doing internal consulting, and the woman's Union representative swept her into a conference room and hatched a scheme. First they called the police (by this time the man had forced his way into the factory). Next, the Union rep and the intended victim switched jackets and headed out the front door to the Union Rep's car and sped off. With the woman safely away (the HR Manager took her car to an undisclosed location,) the executive (accompanied by two large workers) assertively confronted the husband.[22] They told him that his wife was not on the premises, that the police were on the way, and that he was

---

[22]*For the record this was a very inappropriate way to handle this situation (once the woman was safely off the premises) and I do not condone this behavior. The man should have been considered armed and dangerous--confronting such a person is unwise. The executive made himself and the two workers targets. The executive should have waited for police to respond, and probably initiate a lockdown/intruder response for the whole workforce in the meantime.*

trespassing. The police arrived and found that the man was indeed armed and he was charged with trespassing, but at that point the laws were not stringent enough to charge him with carrying a concealed weapon. There were no further incidents.

The most remarkable thing about this story is that nobody had any training in what to do in this situation, and furthermore no one was authorized to intervene, but they did. The workers came together as a community to protect one of their own. Fortunately, we don't have to rely on initiating a response to a threat as it becomes imminent. We will examine how you can plan for an attack and take steps to prevent it. These examples are clearly not based on work-from-home employees, but I use them to illustrate that not all corporations are heartless monsters, and that if you feel your safety or security might be at risk, don't be afraid to reach out and ask your employer for help.

Protecting Yourself/Employees Who Work-From-Home

There is a great deal of information in this book about protecting workers from violence that are not unique to a traditional workplace, but let's take a look at what you can do to protect remote workers specifically:

- **Make the resources that are available to the worker clear and easy to access.** Workers who are in danger of being targeted for violence may feel helpless and may not know what to do if they are in danger. Be sure that you explain all the things the worker can do about a dangerous situation, and how to do them. Many companies have (and yours should have) resources than can literally save the life of someone targeted for violence, including:

  - **Legal Aid.** From getting assistance filing for divorce from an abusive spouse to filing a restraining order against a threatening customer, co-worker, or neighbor, free legal aid is an excellent way for a company to provide protection to employees without interjecting itself into a turbulent situation.

- o **Employee Assistance Plans (EAP).** EAPs are a great way to provide workers with a clearing house of information on violence antecedents like: financial hardship, drug/alcohol abuse counseling, mental health treatment, or even a direct cry for help for protection from violence.

- **Communicate the procedure for reporting a danger.** You should have, and communicate, a hotline for reporting the risk of workplace violence. Ideally, this should be available 24/7 and have the option of reporting the threat online or via text message.

- **Establish "safe travel" protocols.** I have worked for several firms that required me to do a comprehensive travel plan to ensure my safety. Whenever I left my home office (yes, including for lunch,) I would have to telephone my boss when I left the house, telephone him when I reached my destination, do so again when I left my destination, and finally once again when I reached home. If I made any stops in my journey I would have to telephone him when I stopped and started. I thought it was ridiculous until I started traveling to unsafe areas, at which point knowing that someone knew where I was and could send help if needed made me feel a lot better. Oh, and we quickly switched from phone calls to text messages, so it really wasn't much of a burden.

- **Load Emergency Response Apps Onto Smart Phones.** Many smart devices come with emergency response applications that will call 911 and your in-case-of-emergency contacts. I know because my phone has this and I have accidentally called 911. When I explained what happened to the 911 operator and apologized profusely, she explained that it happened so often that they no longer charged for "false 911" calls. She responded that it was better to have 50 accidental calls than to have someone second-guess whether or not to call for help. I think she was just being nice to me because she thought I probably ate lead paint chips with salsa as a child.

- **Be alert to "red flags."** In far too many tragedies, someone invariably says, "I could have told you this would happen..." in Cassandra-esque resignation. There is no such thing as retroactive (or radioactive for that matter) wisdom. The truth of the matter is we see signs of danger, or at the very least signs that something is not quite right, and ignore it. In worker safety we often say: "See something. Say something. Do something."[23] In this case, we need to transform this from a tired, clichéd slogan into a mantra, the driving principle of our work lives. Butt in. Meddle. Ask the uncomfortable question–and don't accept pat answers. We'll explore red flags in greater detail, but for now we'll just deal with some of the red flags that you can detect on a video call:

  - **Black eyes and bruises**. If you see someone with blackened eyes, bruises, abrasions on their face, round or oval bruises on their neck, or wearing so much makeup that they make the Juggalo look like Mennonites, don't be afraid to ask, point blank, how the person got the black eye. And don't be satisfied with old standards like "I walked into a door." I've gotten so drunk that I had to be carried to a rickshaw in New Orleans and transported back to my hotel in said vehicle, and yet I wasn't so drunk that I couldn't negotiate a doorway. Furthermore, I have walked into doors before and I have never blackened my eyes while doing so. Is it possible? I suppose it is, but I have to believe more people have had their eyes blackened by fists than by walking into doors. And don't let the person deflect with a glib response like, "I do Fight Club on

---

[23] *Safety as a field is filled with shitbirds who have an unnatural predilection for slogans. Seriously, these bastards have a sick fetish for slogans.*

Wednesdays," because, let's face it, if they really WERE in a Fight Club, they couldn't talk about it. Press on with the conversation assertively. "No really, what happened? If you are in trouble I want to help," is a great way to show that you are supportive and to put the person on notice that the abuse is obvious, noticed, and that there is hope.

- o **Clothing that covers the neck and arms.** Typically people who are working from home keep their homes at a temperature that is comfortable to them. If someone is wearing a jacket, turtleneck sweater, or similar garment, they may be trying to conceal the types of injuries discussed above. Again, ask about it.

- o **Sudden changes in personality.** Does the person seem jittery when they typically seem calm? Is the person withdrawn when they used to be outgoing? These can also be signs of domestic abuse. I think you know what's coming here–ask them. "Are you feeling okay today? You seem a little different," can be the conversation starter they need.

- **Use distress codes.** Distress codes are one of the best ways to allow an endangered person to call for help without tipping off his or her abuser. The word(s) should be unusual enough that it will be a clear tip off, but not so unusual that it cannot be comfortably used in a sentence. For instance one of my favorite distress codes is "geranium." Someone in trouble could say, "Larry, was it you who were telling me that your wife likes to grow geraniums? I'm thinking about doing that next spring." This is particularly effective if: a) there is no one on the call named Larry (or Larry isn't married) or b) this conversation, while atypical, could conceivably occur in a meeting without arousing suspicion if the abuser is within earshot.

Another key distress code is the silent signal distress call of "I'm trapped." This simple code works like this: first the person in trouble begins by raising her right hand, open-palmed, as if waving. Next he/she folds her thumb into her palm, keeping her fingers closed. And finally lowering her fingers into a fist. This simple three-gesture signal is powerful. Recently, an abducted teen used this signal to alert a passing vehicle. The driver of the other car recognized the signal, notified the police, got the license plate number, and followed the vehicle from a safe distance. The driver of the suspect vehicle was ultimately arrested for kidnapping the teen, who was returned to her parents.

This signal is not widely known and it should be, as it is a crucial part of any anti-violence campaign. This signal should be widely communicated throughout your organization, not just to potential victims but to *everyone*. It is just as important that those in your organization who can summon help understand this code as it is for those who are being victimized.

- **When in doubt, have the police do a wellness check.** If you have a genuine concern that someone who is working at home is in danger, call the police department in the employee's jurisdiction and share your concerns with the police. Be sure you explain why you suspect that the employee is in danger and request that the police make a "wellness check." In the unlikely event that the police in that jurisdiction don't understand what you mean by a "wellness check," explain that you believe that the employee has been, or is likely to be, harmed. Tell the police that you believe that the worker is in imminent risk of becoming a victim of violence.

Andrew Arena is clear about his view of violent crimes vis-a-vis the pandemic restrictions, "I think the lockdowns have certainly had an impact on uptick in violent crimes nationwide. I can't believe domestic violence is down! Most likely it's underreporting or nonreporting," he says.

Summary

While OSHA makes it clear that employers must provide a workplace free of foreseeable hazards, OSHA doesn't even mention one of the most dangerous and lethal threats to workplace safety: workplace violence. Relying on corporations to make protecting workers in a home office a priority is a lot like relying on a fox to guard the henhouse. Furthermore, OSHA has as much as said that it will not go into people's private homes to enforce even the most egregious safety precautions, so effectively the home office can easily be used to castrate OSHA and leave workers in a home office with no safety protections under the law.

Even though there is no OSHA regulation requiring you to take action if a work-from-home employee is in danger, there are things you can do to protect remote workers.

Thought Starters

OSHA's policy on safety in the home office has largely been hands off. What approach should OSHA take to protecting workers from workplace violence that happens outside the traditional workplace?

Is workplace violence foreseeable? Why or why not?

With the overall increase in violence and mental illness, is a corresponding increase in workplace violence inevitable? Why or why not?

How should society balance the right of a worker's privacy with an employers' real or perceived responsibility to protect remote workers?

Chapter 6: Worker Safety in the Gig Economy

For the last three years or so I have been writing articles for Authority magazine. I am complimented for my insightful and thought-provoking questions. I must admit most of the ones that make it to print are really interesting people. The insights from these interviews—across a broad array of topics and people—have taught me both valuable and disturbing things about business and business leaders.

The most upsetting thing I learned in my interviews is the prurient excitement with which many business leaders view the "gig economy."

I am not a gig worker. Sure, I have side hustles—writing books, speaking, sitting on oversight boards—but my primary employment as a W2 employee is at a contract house. I am a contract consultant for one of the major studios and that's all I'll say because of confidentiality considerations. I say this to assure you that I "don't have a dog in this fight."[24] Gig work is not a new phenomenon. People have been working as independent contractors for many years; insurance salespeople and realtors come immediately to mind.

When it comes to the meager protections for employees, gig workers fall through the cracks. They are ideal candidates for being exploited by disreputable employers. But first, some definitions. A "gig worker" is a person that is paid to do a specific task, and while that task could take years, they are essentially "as needed" employees. They are typically treated with the same respect, decorum, and concern reserved for a thrice-used condom. They are the members of the growing, invisible, the Untouchable Caste of employees. In many employers' minds, the gig worker is disposable and not part of the team.

"Jesus can't watch out for everyone so it's best to watch out for yourself"—*Watching Out for Jesus*, The Rave-Ups

While OSHA requires that employers extend protection to I-9 contractors and temporary employees, this protection does not extend to gig workers. Gig workers don't qualify for Workers' Compensation, they have to pay both the employer's and employee's share of social security, and have to pay their own insurance, which is astonishingly costly. What's more, the "Great Resignation" has seen a rise in the number of gig workers. Not everyone thinks gig work is a bad idea, and many greedy and short-sighted captains of industry see it as the future of work. Eventually, gig workers will wise up and either unionize or, at a minimum, raise their prices to compensate for their out-of-pocket costs. But what price can be put on the lives of gig workers who are caught in the crossfire of workplace violence? Do the lives of gig workers even matter, and if so what are we doing to protect

---

[24]*Relax all you animal lovers and cat fanciers, I neither condone nor encourage dog fighting—or*

cockfighting either for that matter, although I still contend that there isn't a chicken alive that I can't beat in a fair fight.

them? The short answer is nothing, so gig workers had better find a way to watch out for themselves. Fortunately, companies who employ everything from over-the-road truckers to consultants have policies designed to protect workers who are working alone, and gig workers can learn much from these safety policies.

Safety For Gig Workers

Years ago, I was managing a fast food restaurant and on five separate occasions, I was solicited by customers to meet to discuss a mysterious business opportunity. I only met with one of the five (he was the editor of a weekly newspaper, had businesscards, and suggested that we meet for lunch and I ultimately became a reporter as a result of that meeting.) The other four were turned off by my Amway deposit. Every one of them presented the opportunity as managing a distribution center, and were eager to discuss the opportunity. Eager, that is, until I told them about the Amway deposit. When they asked for details, I told them "It's simple. You give me $500 cash at the beginning of the meeting, and if the opportunity is legit and not Amway or some similar multi-level marketing scheme, I give the $500 back. But if the mystery business opportunity turns out to be something where I recruit saps to sell overpriced products that nobody wants, then I keep the $500 for my trouble." At this point I would put in a disclaimer that not all multi-level marketing companies are sleazy attempts to prey on the poor and stupid, but I honestly doubt that anyone so employed could afford this book or understand it if they could. I have two relatives who worked for multi-level marketing companies and were neither stupid nor gullible, but they got into the business because they really liked the product and as a distributor they got a terrific discount. Both left the company because their managers were pressuring them to recruit more sales people; it's a shame because I really liked the products.

Tips For Protecting Yourself When Working In A Gig Economy

So whatever you call it—gig work, side hustle, "it beats starving,"

etc,—these workers are not protected as "workers" since each is an independent contractor. Even so, people who work in these types of situations are not powerless to protect themselves, and they really need to take these simple protective measures:

- **Research the client before agreeing to meet with him or her.** When I was young I was laid off by General Motors. The economy of Detroit, my hometown, had tanked, and it seemed like everyone was out to take advantage of job seekers. I had an interview for a District Manager of a national (presumably international) pizza chain. I had all the qualifications listed in the job posting and nailed the interview. The Hiring Manager and Director of Operations said that they were eager to hire me. Then they dropped the hammer. They told me that the training for the position involved me delivering pizzas for six months (for less than minimum wage, as I was eligible for tips,) followed by making pizzas for six months (making minimum wage,) followed by being the "counter man" for a year, then being promoted to Assistant Manager where I would work until a Manager position opened up. I would be expected to manage a branch for "five years or so" at which point I would be given the job I had applied for (and was offered.) I told them that their offer was insane and unsustainable. They painted a glorious picture of how wealthy I was going to be and I told them that I had a family and that my infant child couldn't eat pizza every night—though now she would love such an arrangement.. I was steaming mad until the same thing happened to me three additional times, from managing a furniture store to managing a shoe store. Keep in mind, in each case, I was dealing with national or international chains, and each time they tried the same sleazy con.[25]

The examples I shared here involve a full-time position and, while sleazy, I didn't put myself in any real danger. That hasn't always been the case, however. Once I went to a job interview for a Branch Manager position. I was a strong candidate and once again aced the interview. The office was in disarray and the man from corporate (ostensibly in Chicago) was dressed in sweats. He apologized for his appearance and said he knew that he would be working around a construction site. He made me an offer at an appropriate—even attractive—salary, and told me I could start the following Monday. When I arrived for work, there were no workers in the office and the door was locked. When I asked for Mr. Smithson, a very sketchy character told me that Mr. Smithson went back to Chicago, and that he (not I) was the boss of this location. He explained to me that I and a group of greasy thugs would be selling crappy electronic equipment out of the back of his rickety panel van at various small factories and shops. I refused to get into the van. He kept cajoling me by saying, "But this is everyday money, man." I assume that meant that I got paid everyday, but I still wasn't having any of it. The bottom line in all of this is that I was desperate. Each experience was like a dagger in my heart. Just a quick call to the Better Business Bureau or the local police department would have probably warned me off from these sleazy pus-bags, and today all I would have needed to do is an internet search, or visit Glassdoors.com or a similar site. And remember, the absence of information is in itself a good indication that you should steer clear. Would any of these sleazy creeps try to harm me? Probably not, but John

---

[25]*On a happy footnote, two of the three are out of business, and the other is dangling by a thread; I guess karma is a real thing.*

Wayne Gacey lured his victims to their death under the auspices of a job interview for a lucrative construction job.

- **Tell someone you trust where you will be meeting.** I once traveled to Los Angeles to meet a man who contacted me via LinkedIn. He owned and operated a business creating and administering online safety training, an area in which I have quite a lot of experience. I did my due diligence and he paid for the flight and hotel room so I figured, why not? The plan was for him to take me to his business and we would discuss the possibility of working together. In the morning I was supposed to meet him (he was going to pick me up at my hotel) but he didn't show up. Instead, his colleague—a woman whom I had never talked with or heard about—arrived and said that the man was tied up, (at this point I wasn't sure whether or not she was speaking literally) and asked her to take me to lunch and then drive me to his house where we would meet. This sent my spider sense tingling and I surreptitiously sent my location from my phone to my sister and my daughter. I also checked in regularly on social media. As it turned out, both were delightful people and while our business venture flopped, the three of us remain close to this day. But the point is that the situation could have gone horribly wrong and left me harmed or conned or dead. Letting someone know where I was is a little backward. Yes, if I had been killed the police would have a good idea of who did it and where my corpse could be found, but that isn't protecting oneself. To protect myself I should have let the strangers know that I needed to check in with my office and phoned my sister or my daughter to let them know that I would call them back when the meeting was over.

- **Meet in a public place with a lot of people around.** It's not impossible to attack someone in a crowded restaurant, but it is likely that if someone does, he or she will be apprehended and a security guard, policeman, or good samaritan may provide aid. If someone insists on meeting somewhere privately, politely decline. Remember the Gacy

Gambit and hold your ground. I didn't and nothing bad happened to me, but too many gig workers are so hungry for the work they forget how vulnerable they are to predator and my experience should be seen as the exception, not as the rule

- **Get to the meeting early and let someone know you are meeting with a stranger.** When meeting with a stranger, get there early. This is a classic organized crime survival technique. Go to the meeting location and scout it out. Find the restrooms and alternate exits and tell someone—a waitress, a bartender, a security guard, a host/hostess—that you are meeting with someone you don't know. Make it clear that if at any time you look as if you are alarmed, fearful, or otherwise in danger, the individual should call the police and not let you leave with the person. It's also wise to have a duress code—something you can say to a server that will tip them off that you are in danger (of course you need to establish this first.) "Is there any chance you serve quail," for example, is a good duress code. It is unique enough that the server is likely to note that something is amiss, but not so obvious that it will trigger a violent reaction from the stranger you are meeting. By the way, this particular tip also works well in on-line dating situations. Remember, no matter how nice a person seems in text messages, emails, or even on phone calls, serial rapists and killers are especially adept at telling vulnerable prospective victims exactly what they need to hear to disarm suspicion.

- **Don't go with the person to a third location.** I've violated this rule many, MANY times—I was young, stupid, and well…let's just say "amorous" in my younger days—but going to a third location increases the likelihood of something bad happening to you. You can avoid this by asking the prospective client for an itinerary for your day. If the prospect refuses, you have a valid reason for passing on the meeting.

- **Create a travel safety plan.** Whether or not you have a specific itinerary, you should create a comprehensive plan from the moment you leave your house until you arrive safely home. Document when you expect to leave a location, the route you will take to the next location and, if you are going to make any stops, where will they be and how long will you be stopped. Sounds ridiculous? Maybe, but plenty of victims would not have been harmed had they made and followed a simple safety plan.

- **Check in at all stops.** Leave a copy of the plan with someone you trust—a friend, a business partner, a family member—and call or text message (calling is better, remember anyone can take your phone and text while pretending to be you) at regular intervals, and always when you make a stop or a detour.

- **Use your smartphone to send your exact location to a trusted party.** Most smart devices allow you to send your location to one or more of your contacts. I know this first hand because I have accidentally left my friends quizzical, having sent my location to them with no explanation.

- **Photograph the person or persons with whom you will be meeting.** This may sound strange, but it is wise to photograph the person with whom you are meeting. Photographing the person does two things: 1) It puts the person on notice that you understand that the person is a stranger and should harm come to you the police will likely be able to retrieve the photo, and 2) while it may not prevent you from being harmed it tends to be a deterrent. Explain to them that having just met them, you want to make sure that you are safe. Additionally, ask to see some form of picture identification (not merely a business card. I was once in my college bookstore where the empty suit in line in front of me, when asked for ID, produced a Ford business card. The clerk, a college co-ed who looked to be about 18, refused the "ID" telling the man that she needed to see a government issued

90

identification with his picture on it. The man was enraged and indignant and told her that he didn't have any other ID. He screamed at her that the business card was from one of the most prestigious Fortune-500 companies and it proved who he was. Finally, she calmly said, "no, that is a piece of cardboard with SOMEONE's name on it." I told him that I was out of time and patience with him. He turned to me red faced and sputtered, "Oh yeah, tough guy, what are you going to do about it?" I smiled and waved the campus policeman (the police were city police with full police authority!) over. I told the policeman what the man had done and then I asked him how the officer thought the man traveled to the bookstore. The policeman asked the man where he was parked and the indignant buffoon told the police officer without realizing that he had confessed to driving without a license. Just when you think you have people figured out they just keep getting dumber. This just illustrates that somebody who is trying to bully you into giving up on your safety may try just about anything to get you to give up; don't give up.

- **Photograph the license plate of the vehicle they are driving.** This is another tip that may put off a stranger, but remember the Gacy Gambit.[26] From Ted Bundy to JW Gacy, the victims had one thing in common—they trusted their attacker. You don't need to be confrontational about taking photos, simply explain that since you've just met, you will feel better about the meeting if your associates know that the person is who he or she claims to be, and once you have snapped a picture the photo goes into the cloud and you can relax. This is the kind of thing you can laugh about years later when the person has become a trusted friend or client, or it is the kind of thing that warns you about a difficult client; either way you win.

---

[26]*This is a term I made up, at least I think I did. The Gacy Gambit refers to John Wayne Gacy's habit of luring victims to his house under the guise of a job interview. Gacy was betting that young men would disregard the obvious danger of going to a stranger's house in pursuit of a lucrative job in construction.*

- **If anything feels weird, get out of there.** I was once approached by a regular customer who told me that he had a great job opportunity that he wanted to discuss with me over dinner. He was vague and evasive, but since we would be meeting at a restaurant I didn't feel I was in danger of anything more than wasting my time. I agreed and met him at the restaurant. When he arrived, he told me there was a change of plans, that we could take his car and go to his friend's house. I told him politely that I wasn't going to his friend's house. This was supposed to be a business meeting over dinner, and that was all I had agreed to. At first he tried to smooth talk me (his friend really knew the details of the deal, his friend was on a call with his overseas partners, his friend's neighborhood didn't have a lot of parking spaces so it was better to take one car, etc.) I was not swayed. I told him to have a seat and tell me what he knew about the deal and if I had questions we could call his friend. Then he got irritated and told me that I was screwing up the chance of a lifetime. I told him maybe, but so far I hadn't heard a single detail of this supposed business venture and I wasn't about to go one step further until I did. Then, he got angry. He shouted at me that I had wasted his time and dragged him out to the restaurant for nothing. I stayed calm and reminded him that this was all his idea; every single detail, right down to this specific restaurant. I told him that the whole situation started to feel fishy and I didn't want any part of it. I don't know what this thing was about, but I can tell you this, the man had been a regular customer at the restaurant where I was a manager, but I never saw him again after that night. The situation was probably harmless, but I wasn't walking into an ambush.

Summary

Gig workers occupy the limbo that exists between full-time employees and independent vendors. As it stands, OSHA does not see gig workers as employees of their customers and therefore said workers are beyond the purview of OSHA. If someone kills a gig worker in a place of business or even in his or her home office, the Bureau of Labor Statistics would not consider it a workplace homicide.

One of the keys to keeping safe when you are working alone, working a side-hustle or a gig, or just meeting with someone for the first time is to do your homework. Do an internet search on the person and company (remember to check sex offender registries, absconders from justice databases, and criminal offender websites. More on this later.)

Always having a travel plan and checking in with someone you trust is critical to protecting yourself against violence.

Thought Starters

Should gig workers be given the same legal entitlement to a safe work environment as traditional workers? Why or why not?

What, if any, responsibility do regulatory agencies have to protect gig workers?

Should health insurance cease to be linked to employment? Why or why not?

What, besides your location, do you think you should provide to your associates when meeting with someone new?

If you were asked for identification and photographed by someone you wanted to hire, would that be enough for you to decline their candidacy for a gig or a job?

Why is it so important to have a travel plan and to stick to it when meeting someone for the first time?

Stop. Don't Shoot!

Chapter 7: Preventing Workplace Violence and Rampage Attacks Begins With Recruiting and Hiring

People are primates and primates are violent creatures. Any of you who have dated a chimp with a drinking problem knows just how dangerous primates can be. And seriously, why are you dating a chimp? Bonobos are the only creatures aside from humans who are known to copulate for fun, stress relief, or to make animal photographers squirm. I'm not telling you how to live your life here, but given the choice between dating a chimp or a bonobo I think that bonobo is the way to go; it's like the old saying, "once you've gone bonobo you've really made so many poor life choices that you couldn't go back even if you wanted to, and frankly why would you?" At least you're not a "Cat Fancier." Chimps also don't take criticism well, but that's for another book. What does all this have to do with preventing workplace violence? A lot of men are a lot more chimp than bonobo; push the wrong buttons and you end up with a broken jaw.

It's impossible to completely prevent workplace violence—

the terrifying reality is if a rampage killer wants to kill people in your workplace, he will likely succeed. and unless you have planned very carefully for such an eventuality, there is little you can do to stop a carefully planned and executed attack. But you *can* greatly reduce the risk of an incidence of workplace violence through some simple changes to your Company policies.

Prevention Begins with Recruiting

I know that I literally just said that preventing workplace violence begins with hiring, but hiring begins with recruiting. If that confuses, befuddles, vexes, or perplexes any of you, feel free to rephrase it when you write your own damned book, but otherwise feel the hurt and let it go. Throughout this chapter I will use the pronoun "you." "You" could be a Human Resource Vice President, or "you" could be a supervisor, or "you"could be a coworker, or "you"could be a potential victim. "You" could even mean you.

For those of you still reading, a good way to avoid a workplace shooting is to avoid hiring people who are unstable and/or who demonstrate a pattern of violent behavior. In this day where people blithely post outrageous and ominous threatening statements that provide a hidden glimpse into their personalities all over the internet, it's now easier than ever to legally gain information on an individual's mental state and volatility.

Everyone has (at least) two faces: the one we show to ourselves and the one we show to recruiters and potential employers. Even as individuals try to conceal embarrassing posts, it is still possible to gain important insights. Here are some potential red flags that are worth considering, as you read through them remember there are two conditions for which you are screening 1) someone who is at high risk of committing workplace violence and 2) someone who is a likely victim of workplace violence. Note that a company shouldn't dismiss a good candidate simply because of the presence of a single red flag—then again these red flags should be strongly considered before hiring (or even interviewing) a candidate— instead look for patterns and follow your gut; you probably already know the candidate that will be a problem employee.:

- **Hate speech.** This should be fairly obvious, but it can be surprisingly common for an individual to post an overt (or thinly veiled) racial slur, ethnic insult, or negative comment indicating bigotry toward one or more subpopulations. This isn't a call for people to be politically correct to a nauseating extent, but if a candidate is comfortable enough to attack a protected class in public posts, he or she probably lacks the judgment of a baboon with late stage syphilis, and ultimately these bigotries will likely manifest in the workplace. A person who allows his or her contacts to post hate speech comments unchallenged on his or her posts is also a red flag; as the adage goes, birds of a feather flock together.

- **Belligerence.** Some people enjoy provoking others; I do, for example, but that is a major part of my job. I have to use provocation to move people out of their comfort zones (the irony of this particular bullet point is not lost on me) so that they can change. But the accounting clerk that you are considering probably isn't being belligerent to make the math work, so a belligerent tone or a pattern of belligerent posts should be weighed against the job and its requirements. I find the sheer number of belligerent social maladroits that dismiss the person interviewing them as unimportant interesting; they are seemingly oblivious to the fact that the job of the first few people interacting with them, their resumés, or their social media presence is to weed out the weirdos.

- **Volatility.** Even a saint can be pushed to the breaking point and post or say something that he or she wished they hadn't, but what can be really telling is when a person shifts from mildly argumentative to the equivalent of a screaming, frothy rage. This "flick a switch" going from zero to raging, gaping maniac (not my first choice of word) is a strong red flag. Even though we know that people often act online in a way that they would never act in person, they still secretly or silently harbor these feelings strongly enough to post them in a public forum and the right stimuli could set them off; at the very least these candidates lack the judgment that most people would like to see in an employee.

- **Obsession with guns**. This might seem obvious to some and unfair to others. I have a social contact who almost exclusively posts photos of automatic weapons. Another is a self-described gun nut. In and of themselves, these two would seem to be people you don't want to hire. In fact, one of them is in ROTC and the other is an artist that draws weapons for a popular single-shooter video game and requires the guns for research for his job. Neither of them is belligerent or exhibits any violent tendencies; again these are indicators and have to be considered in a larger context with the other red flags.

- **Obsession with violent events**. Whenever there is a high-profile rampage attack, the social networks are littered with posts relative to the event. But there are also individuals who post memes, articles, or statements that suggest if not an obsession with violence, a keen interest in it. Personally, I would also steer clear of people who post pictures of their cats dressed in holiday costumes—they may not be dangerous or violent, but I'm not going to share a cube with them.[27]

- **Hostility toward an ex-partner**. Personally, I don't trust anyone who has an amicable relationship with their ex-lover or ex-spouse, when people used to ask me if I was still friends with my ex-wife I would simply tell them that if we got along we would probably still be married.[28] Of course there are actually some couples who can be civil with their ex-partners but I still have my doubts. In any case, posting hateful rants for all the world to see makes me question their judgment, if not their mental stability.

---

[27] *For the record, many of my best friends are cats so I am not anti-cat. Relax man, it is not always about you.*

[28] *Instead of telling the nosy bastards to mind their own businesses*

- **"It's Complicated" Relationship Status**. Tread lightly here. In many countries, it is illegal to ask about, or to use as a criterion for hiring, a candidate's marital status, and that is not what I am suggesting. But the response "it's complicated" could indicate marital strife, difficulties with an on-again-off-again partner, marriage to a semiaquatic mammal, or a variety of situations that raise a red flag. Then again, it could indicate a relationship that is completely innocuous and in no way predictive of workplace violence. The point being is that any vagueness that could indicate a propensity for future workplace violence needs to be considered for the purposes of future heightened awareness should you hire the person, not as a criterion for such a hire.

- **Excessive alcohol use.** Is there a preponderance of posts relating to alcohol use? Does the candidate proudly post the details (at least what they can remember) of the previous weekend's bender? Are the pictures (disproportionately) of alcoholic drinks or of social events where alcohol is served? Does the candidate often check in at bars or parties? In most of the workplace violence episodes, alcohol is involved. The perfect formula for a workplace single shooter event is an unhappy relationship + quick access to a firearm + mental illness with violent tendency + alcohol. Clearly not everyone who enjoys drinking is going to be a mad-dog killer, but it's easier to avoid hiring someone than hiring someone and having to fire them, or worse yet force them out of the company. It's important to use your judgment here; a lot of people post pictures of vacations, holiday celebrations, weddings, or other festive occasions (even blowing off steam with friends at a bar) and this doesn't mean that you shouldn't hire them. On the other hand, if the majority of the posts are about how wasted they got before grocery shopping or on the way to work, it should give you pause.

- **An overall negative outlook.** Everybody gets negative once in a while, but as you read through a candidate's posts, do they seem overly angry, depressed, or just seem to view the world as filled with personal injustices and unpleasantness? If so, how qualified does Eeyore have to be for you to say, "Gosh darn it, this candidate's post makes ME depressed but I still want 'em on my team?"

Negativity can be contagious, and it can spread with alarming speed. Once negativity takes root, it can poison a corporate culture. A person with a negative outlook is also less resilient, which correlates to more absenteeism and difficulty rebounding from personal or professional setbacks. Even if the person isn't a potential killer, who wants to have this person at the company picnic?

- **No social media presence.** In an age when grandparents have Facebook pages and Twitter accounts, it is practically unheard of for someone under the age of 70 to be completely absent from social media. If someone doesn't have any social media accounts, it may indicate that they have deleted the accounts or are using a pseudonym. This is hardly damning; the person may merely want to get rid of the public displays of youthful indiscretions. My Facebook page is festooned with posts of me drinking, spewing obscenities (some of which I made up[29]) and dubious check-ins. It makes sense that people are going to post a fancy mixed drink or being under the beverage with friends, I like people to have a good idea who they're dealing with, plus as an author who is known for his poison-pen and tongue dripping venom, I get away with a lot more than most. As for your average candidate, again, it shouldn't be a deal breaker but should be considered another possible indicator. If you were considering bringing me aboard when you started reading, some of you may have since changed your mind. It's just as well, I am pretty much unemployable—I am not the one who got away, I am the bullet that was dodged.

- **Membership in—or sympathy for—domestic terrorist or hate groups.** After the U.S. Capital was stormed and armed groups tried to overthrow the Federal Government by disrupting the certification of Joe Biden as President, many people in The United States began to take domestic terrorism much more seriously. Even after the attack on the Federal building in Oklahoma City in the 1990s, many Americans dismissed domestic terrorists as an overstatement—in the minds of many, these domestic terrorists were disorganized, loners, and sort of pathetic lunatics. January 6, 2021 changed all that. And because social media is a primary recruiting, communicating, and planning tool, companies can no longer ignore members or sympathizers of these groups. According to Andrew Arena, "Obviously right-wing extremists are a threat for violence within the agitated, political landscape we face today.[30] However, they seem to be more of a threat for a planned and focused event. Obviously, extremist groups do spawn "lone wolf" attacks. This is true all along the political and religious spectrum.`` A member of such an organization is: a) accustomed to and comfortable with using violence to

---

[29]*Patent pending...fingers crossed*
[30]*Exclusive interview with Andrew Arena by Phil La Duke*

resolve conflicts b) emboldened by the perceived support of their comrades and sympathizers, and c) generally not shy about spouting their rhetoric. At this point in time, there have been no rampage attacks known to have been perpetrated by a member of these domestic terrorist groups, but the possibility of continuing attacks normalizing violence, particularly gun violence, as a way to resolve conflicts or perceived grievances make the possibility much greater than ever before.

Again, none of these factors alone identifies a dangerous individual, but each one provides an important piece of the puzzle that you really need when you hire a person, and you need that information BEFORE you bring the person in for an interview.

All of this sounds like a lot of work and it can be, but it is far less time-consuming and gut-wrenching than telling the loved ones of someone murdered in your workplace that you could have prevented the death, but it was just too much darned work (don't worry, I'm sure they will understand and may even take comfort in your kind words of condolences.)

I've heard arguments that social media is protected speech, and a person has every right to post whatever he or she pleases. It's a fair point, but people too often believe that freedom of speech includes protection from the consequences of the malodorous dreck spewing from your mouth. Social media has given a forum for every crackpot conspiracy theorist and domestic terrorist to spew their misguided nonsense. You do have the right to say (within limits) what you want. Most people don't read the social networks' terms of services and these terms of service often (almost always) severely curtail exactly the types of things you can and can't say. And while many forms of social media have tightened restrictions on what is allowed on their sites, they scarcely do enough. But even if social media didn't have anything in place, there is nothing stopping people from thinking that you're a complete mouth-breathing, drooling asshat. Sadly of all the rights that people choose to exercise, too few exercise their right to remain silent.

Background Checks

Before we get into background checks, we should review what the U.S. Federal Equal Opportunity Commission has to say on the subject, because, let's face it, violating the law is wrong even when the intent is to protect your workers. The EOC says: "Federal law does not prohibit employers from asking about your criminal history. But, federal EEO laws do prohibit employers from discriminating when they use criminal history information. Using criminal history information to make employment decisions may violate Title VII of the Civil Rights Act of 1964, as amended (Title VII).

- Title VII prohibits employers from treating people with similar criminal records differently because of their race, national origin, or another Title VII-protected characteristic (which includes color, sex, and religion).

- Title VII prohibits employers from using policies or practices that screen individuals based on criminal history information if:

    o they significantly disadvantage Title VII- protected individuals such as African Americans and Hispanics; AND they do not help the employer accurately decide if the person is likely to be a responsible, reliable, or safe employee.

    o They do not help the employer accurately decide if the person is likely to be a responsible, reliable, or safe employee."[31]

Okay, so another disclaimer, I am not a lawyer (I don't even play one on TV.) But having said that, what this quote means is that you have every right to ask about criminal history, restraining orders, arrests, etc. as long as you don't ask one protected class more frequently than another. So IF you look into someone's criminal

---

[31] *Source: https://eeoc,gov/laws/practices/inquireis_arrest_conviction.com*

and arrest records, you should be doing it for ALL candidates for that position, and can defend against claims that you are singling out someone because of their race, religion, country of origin, or similar protected class, AND that you are doing the investigation in a good faith effort to ensure the safety of your employees, which given the context of this investigation, i.e. to reduce the risk of hiring someone with a history of violent behavior that could spill over into the workplace, should not be hard to do. Let's face it, if you were to close your eyes and picture your average domestic abuser, your picture would likely be wrong. The fact is, except for the fact that the population is overwhelmingly male, it is nearly impossible to identify a domestic abuser by looks alone.

In the rush to fill a position, some employers will skip background checks. A background check is an important step in the hiring process. Some companies, citing the expense, will only do background checks on candidates who are above a certain pay grade. Ironically, the incidences of disgruntled executives returning to a workplace to kill indiscriminately are all but unheard of. When considering the expense of a background check, consider the cost of having a sociopath on the payroll. Companies can never underestimate the dangers of skipping background checks. Background checks should include:

- **Court records.**[32] Does the candidate have a restraining order against him or her, or has the candidate filed for a restraining order against someone else? This is easy information to obtain and it is a big red flag that the candidate is either capable of violence or has a relationship with someone who is potentially dangerous. filing a restraining order against someone could mean that the candidate is a victim (and this should not be a criterion for hiring) or it could be a person who retaliates against someone he has victimized. Incidents of domestic abuse should be given particular scrutiny, as they are often a causative factor in rampage attacks.

---

[32]Source:https://www.hrw.org/reports/2007/us0907/5.htm#:~:text=Today%20all%2050%20states%20and,register%2C%20and%20for%20how%20long.

- **Arrest Record.** Has the candidate been arrested (but perhaps not charged) for violent crimes, particularly for domestic violence? Why domestic violence? Let's not forget that a leading cause of rampage attack fatalities is domestic disputes and more likely than not,the woman associated with the case will be a victim.

- **Online Registries.** Most people are aware that all of the states in the U.S. have a registry of sex offenders (as does the Distric of Columbia) as required by the U.S. Federal Government. Most, if not all, states also maintain a registry of individuals who have been convicted of a crime (that may or may not constitute a sex crime) and a database of people who have "absconded from justice" (skipped bail.)

There are a couple of factors that you should remember when reviewing these registries:

1. The registry only tells you the crimes of which the individual has been convicted, and while they will include "special circumstances" (mitigating circumstances that make a crime more serious) they do not tell you what the person was actually arrested for—a person on the registry for public urination may actually have been arrested for lewd and lascivious conduct. The crime that makes the registry is often the result of a plea bargain to a lesser charge. You can only view these registries through the lens of the best-case scenario.

2. Remember that the story you hear from the candidate is going to be sanitized to make the crime seem justified, even reasonable. Personally, I wouldn't hire anyone on the sex offender list and I wouldn't be all that crazy about hiring an ex-con. For what it's worth, I don't think everyone deserves a second chance, but if you do, keep this information in mind.

3. The lack of a criminal record is not proof of a lack of criminal activity—we've all exceeded the speed limit, rolled through a stop sign, engaged in road rage, or robbed

the occasional party store. Just because someone got away with a crime doesn't mean the person hasn't committed one (or more.)

- **Criminal Record.** A criminal record doesn't mean that the person is prone to violence, however, if the person has lied about his or her criminal conviction it is an indicator of the person's character. We will address the legality of discriminating against people with arrest charges and criminal records in the following extremely boring section on labor law. Note: the EOC has different rules governing arrest and conviction records:

Difference Between Arrest Records and Conviction Records

The fact that an individual was arrested is not proof that he or she engaged in criminal conduct. Therefore, an individual's arrest record standing alone may not be used by an employer to take a negative employment action (e.g., not hiring, firing, or suspending an applicant or employee.) However, an arrest record may trigger an inquiry into whether the conduct underlying the arrest justifies such action.

In contrast, a conviction record will usually be sufficient to demonstrate that a person engaged in particular criminal conduct. In certain circumstances, however, there may be reasons for an employer not to rely on the conviction record alone when making an employment decision.

Several states' laws limit employers' use of arrest and conviction records to make employment decisions. These laws may prohibit employers from asking about arrest records or require employers to wait until late in the hiring process to ask about conviction records. If you have questions about these kinds of laws, you should contact your State Fair Employment Agency for more information.[33]

---

[33]*For more information on the laws governing criminal background checks go to*
*https://www.eeoc.gov/eeoc/newsroom/wysk/arrest_conviction_records.c*fm

- **History of Incarceration.** Even individuals who have been incarcerated for non-violent offenses can often become indoctrinated into a culture of violence as a direct result of prolonged incarceration. This is not to say that you shouldn't hire an ex-convict, however, it is another indicator that the person may have violent tendencies, and you need to consider this in the context of all facets of the person's personality and background. I could go on and on about the many convicted felons who went on to become sterling citizens, but then this book isn't intended to protect you from reformed convicts like Jean Valjean; if you are looking for that read Les Miserables.

- **Military Discharge Status.** I resolutely believe that we owe a tremendous debt to our veterans, but not all veterans are choir boys. When it came to burying my ex-father-in-law, it came to light that he was not an "honorary discharged veteran" and therefore not eligible for certain benefits, like for instance, a military burial. He had received a "general discharge" after beating the snot out of a superior. Another known associate of mine also received a general discharge when the camp commander told him "you don't like being here and we don't want you here so if you want to go we'll discharge you." He eagerly accepted and left the service two months early (if you are asking what kind of idiot avoids an honorable discharge with only two months left on his bit…. I don't have the answers you seek.)
Harold B. Wolford of the Delaware Gazette does an excellent job of deciphering the often confusing types of military discharges:

"The various branches of the United States military may have terms for these discharges that are unique to that service, whether used formally or informally…Brief explanations of military discharges are as follows:

1. **Honorable discharge.** This is the highest discharge a military member can receive. It indicates the service

member performed duties well, faithfully executed the mission, and was an asset to the branch of the military where the member served.

2. **General discharge under honorable conditions**. This type of military administrative discharge is motivated by different things depending on the branch of service. The overall conduct of the military member may have been exemplary in some areas, but other areas of misconduct or failure to adapt to the military environment may have resulted in such a discharge.

   The separation paperwork for these military discharges may be quite specific about the reasons for the discharge, so while it's not stigmatized the same as a dishonorable discharge, the general discharge under honorable conditions may still hurt the veteran in some ways where a DD Form 214 Report of Discharge is required for employment or other reasons.

   Depending on the severity of the problems mentioned in the DD Form 214, the veteran may receive a reenlistment code that determines the service member's eligibility for any future military service.

3. **Other than honorable (OTH) discharge**. This is the most severe of the administrative discharges (which do not require a court-martial). Reasons for the OTH discharge may depend on the severity of the offenses, how a particular branch of the military has traditionally handled such issues, and other variables.
   Security violations, trouble with civilian authorities, assault, drug possession or various degrees of drug violations or other problems could all potentially motivate an other than honorable discharge. The OTH discharge should be considered to be a barrier to future military service.

4. **Bad conduct discharges**. A bad conduct discharge comes as the result of a court-martial and may be followed by prison time depending on the nature and severity of the conduct. This type of military discharge is not considered an administrative one and is a barrier to future military service.

5. **Dishonorable discharge.** This is the most punitive of all military discharges and is given as the result of a court-martial. Desertion, murder, fraud, and other crimes performed in uniform can result in court-martial proceedings that lead to a dishonorable discharge. No military benefits or future military service is possible with a military discharge characterized as dishonorable.

6. **Other military discharges**. A new recruit that cannot complete basic training, adapt to the military environment while in basic training or tech school, or otherwise is unable or unwilling to complete the initial phases of training before moving out of training and into "permanent party" status would be given an entry-level discharge or entry-level separation depending on the branch of military service.

   These separations generally happen before the new recruit has served more than 180 days. These are not considered "good" or "bad" discharges, the recruit is not considered a veteran, and those receiving entry level separations are not eligible for benefits.

7. **A medical discharge** may be given to service members who become sick or injured to the point where military duty is no longer possible based on a medical evaluation of the medical condition. This process can be lengthy and may or may not be appealed depending on a variety of factors. Military members who receive medical discharges should apply for VA compensation for service-connected medical issues, especially those that resulted in the discharge.

Sometimes, depending on the branch of military service, a situation may require the separation of a new recruit or permanent party military member "for the convenience of the government." This type of discharge is done at the discretion of the branch of service involved and is not considered a common or routine practice."[34] So while hiring a vet is an admirable thing to do, hiring a vet that has not been honorably discharged is another red flag that you should consider.

- **Employment History.** Are there significant gaps in the person's work history? These could indicate incarceration or commitment to a mental institution. Do the companies seem reticent about discussing the circumstances of the person's departure from the company? If possible, talk to the candidate's manager; he or she will likely be candid regarding whether or not the candidate is capable of committing workplace violence. Be careful not to put too much stock in a single gap or even several short gaps. It is becoming more commonplace for a person to quit a job to care for a sick or elderly parent, take care of small children, or many other innocuous reasons. I have considered it myself, but my creditors were most insistent that I continue working. Some people leave toxic work environments— because they feared that a co-worker could have been a target (or perpetrator) of workplace violence, the candidate decided to quit his or her job despite not having another job already arranged. But at the risk of sounding repetitive (did I say that already?) this is a single indicator in a long line of indicators.

- **Credit History.** People assume I am rich. Not because I am particularly urbane or cultured, well dressed, nor because I drive a nice car. No, people assume I am rich because I write so much. Writing books (or worse yet magazine articles) is not the golden ticket to wealth. My

---

[34]*Source: https://www.delgazette.com/opinion/88217/types-of-military-discharges-explained*

experience is one probably makes more money reading books than writing them, but c'est la vie. Credit checks are an increasingly common part of the background check, and it can provide important clues to potential perpetrators or victims of a single shooter event. Money problems rank very high in the list of causes of marital (or nontraditional spousal partnership) problems and are quite often a trigger for domestic violence. But if you are going to use this information to ascertain criminal acts, you should be aware of the EOC's Consumer Protections and Criminal Background Checks guidelines:

- o "Employers that obtain an applicant's or employee's criminal history information from consumer reporting agencies (CRAs) also must follow the Fair Credit Reporting Act (FCRA). For example, FCRA requires employers to:

  - Get your permission before asking a CRA for a criminal history report;

  - Give the candidate a copy of the report and a summary of their rights under FCRA before taking a negative employment action based on information in the report.

  - Send you certain notices if it decides not to hire or promote you based on the information in the CRA report."[35]

- **References.** Some people view asking for references as a waste of time; after all, what kind of social misfit would

---

[35] *If you would like to know more about FCRA, visit the Federal Trade Commission's (FTC) website (the Federal agency that enforces FRCA). Or contact the FTC at 1-888-FTC-HELP (1-800-832-4357; TTY: 1-866-653-4261*

give the names of someone who will give them a bad reference? Precisely the kind who might shoot up your office and destroy that snowglobe your boss brought you back from his trip to Des Moines (don't expect the cheap bastard to replace it.) I have checked references for candidates only to find out that the person listed as a reference didn't know or gave an out-and-out bad reference for the potential hire. Ask the reference about how the candidate handles stress, or even if they believe that the candidate is capable of violence, or if there is anyone in the candidate's life that might be violent and wish to harm the candidate. Anonymity breeds candor. As for me, I once told a person that called me for a reference on a very good friend of mine that said friend was deceased. The reference-checker asked if I could give a reference for him, to which I replied, "Who? Ron? He's dead; he's been dead." Miraculously, he got the job (after I told the reference-checker that I was joking and we had a good laugh) but I think this anecdote illustrates nicely that references are a wildcard, and that no one in their right mind should list me as a reference.[36]

- **Google Searches and Social Media Reviews**. It's always surprising how much information you can get from a simple search on the web. As a reporter and contributor to numerous magazines, I have something of a reputation for being able to quickly and accurately get information. My secret? Google. I don't pay for information, but it's not a bad idea to do so. Andrew Arena is a lawyer and his take on this is significant, "Social media monitoring has been used traditionally for marketing purposes, but more companies are using these tools to identify potential safety issues. We all seem to live our lives out in the universe of social media. In hindsight, many of these shooters foretold their actions on social media. Imagine if we could see it coming!"Remember to dig deep in your Google searches.

---

[36]*Source:* https://www.eeoc.gov.laws/practices_arrest_conviction.cfm

Professional cleaners will simply add so much new (and usually inane) information that a cursory glance won't reveal a person's arrest for having carnal knowledge of a dead raccoon because it will be so deeply buried that you are unlikely to find it unless you Google "sex"+"dead raccoon." This is in no way any attempt to denigrate those of you with a predilection toward raccoon necrophilia, but isn't that something you would like to learn about a candidate BEFORE you hire someone? On a related note, I read a book of bizarre news stories culled from newspapers throughout the world. Perhaps my favorite was a man who defended himself against animal cruelty charges when police caught him in the act of violating the carcass of a dead raccoon by claiming in court that "the raccoon was dead when I found it." Personally, I would have just paid the fine.

- **Drug Screening.** In this day and age where marijuana is increasingly legal, companies are finding it of lesser and lesser value to conduct drug screening. In the words of one Human Resources Vice President, "hardly anyone fails." But here is the problem with this thinking: we are in the midst of an opioid epidemic and drug addicts are known for their lack of trustworthiness (trust me, I was married to one.) There is also another good reason to conduct drug testing: before the test the candidate is required to list all the drugs he or she is taking (prescription, over the counter, or recreational.) If the candidate fails to disclose this information and the presence of undisclosed drugs are detected, it is grounds for dismissal. Better yet, having this information in advance allows you to choose not to hire the liar. Why is it so important to understand what drugs (and by the way you, should have your provider of drug tests screen for masking agents as well) a candidate is taking? Because many mentally ill individuals use recreational drugs to self-medicate and THAT is worth knowing. Additionally, knowing what medications an employee takes can be helpful if that employee has any medical emergencies while on the job site.

I worked for a company that had five different clients that required my firm to randomly test the employees for drugs. I used to joke that since I worked for all five clients (and therefore was randomly tested once or twice a month,) I kept a mason jar of pee in my refrigerator because I get "randomly" selected so often that it just saved time. An added benefit was it kept guests in my home from getting too comfortable helping themselves to things in my

refrigerator. Hey, life is short; I might as well enjoy it.

Summary

While many will argue that it's impossible to completely prevent workplace violence, those people are simpletons. Yes, in a literal sense, we cannot, beyond all uncertainty, guarantee that our workplace will never be the location of a rampage killing, but that doesn't mean we shouldn't try. We needn't live in a constant state of anxiety, especially when there are so many simple steps we can take to assess the risk of an attack on our workplaces, plan for the unlikely scenario that a rampaging killer will target our workforce, and ultimately greatly decrease the likelihood of an incidence of workplace violence through some simple changes to company policies.

It can be difficult to identify those individuals who are prospective killers, but weeding out the weirdos begins before the first interview. For example, background checks used to be costly and time consuming, but now they are easy to obtain and inexpensive, making them a useful tool.

Other insights into a candidate's life can be obtained by reviewing the individual's social media or absence of social media use. A routine check of the sex offenders list, offender tracking databases, domestic violence databases, and absconders from justice website, are excellent places to look for people who you probably don't want to hire.

Thought Starters

If a candidate's employment history, particularly the circumstances of the employee's departure from previous positions, are so important, why do so many employers fail to do an adequate job in thoroughly investigating this area?

Social media is ubiquitous and many people routinely disclose intimate details that they would never disclose to a potential employer. What inferences would you expect to draw from a person with absolutely no social media presence?

The law limits what an employer can ask in pre-employment interviews, do you think this is a good idea? Why or why not?

Does an employer have an ethical responsibility to disclose why they did not extend an offer of employment to a candidate?

Why or why not?

Is it okay to tell a "white lie," for example, say you left a job in October when you actually left in August, on your résumé? Why or why not?

Is a thorough and complete background check before an interview really worth it? Why or why not?

Chapter 8: Interviewing A Candidate

Interviewing a candidate is the best way to get to know them in a short amount of time. Learning about the person's timeliness, dress, mannerisms, tone of voice, and just your gut feeling about a candidate may prove invaluable. In addition to the questions you would normally ask, you should ask questions that provide you with insight into the person's personality. Ask open-ended questions like the following to gain information that you can use (legally and ethically) to avoid hiring someone who will likely engage in workplace violence or make your company a target for a rampage attack:

- Tell me about a time when you had an altercation with a coworker, how did you react?

- Have you ever felt threatened or in danger of being harmed by a coworker, supervisor, or customer? If so how did you handle that situation., and if not, hypothetically speaking how would you handle a situation like this?

- Have you ever witnessed a security breach, suspicious behavior, or escalating hostility? How did you (or would you) handle this situation?

I literally could write a book about the stupid things people say in job interviews (but I wrote this one and four others instead.) If you want to hear them, buy me a beer and get comfortable.

Keep in mind that one of the most difficult things in a job interview is determining whether or not the person is a duplicitous, pathological liar. In his June 2016 article for *Psychology Today, 6 Ways to Detect a Liar,* Dr. Gregory L. Jantz offers some insightful ways to tell if someone is being completely truthful. According to Jantz, 80% of lies go undetected,[37] but if that is true, can we really believe him? He might be one of the people who is lying to us! It's like a blog post I wrote titled "60% of statistics are made up." Angry dullards with furrowed brows angrily hammered out hate mail, insisting that I tell them the source of this statistic. Assuming Jantz isn't lying, Jantz asserts that the all too common practice of a child lying about eating candy before dinner (and presumably other inconsequential untruths) set the pattern for lying in later life. "This opportunity-cost processes that children go through to avoid getting in trouble sets the foundation for a pattern of lying in the future" notes Jantz. And while Jantz claims that "people will always get away with lying, most lies are pretty easy to spot if you know how to read the signs.

Jantz suggests that we start by asking some neutral questions, by this he means questions that all but the most sociopathic creeps would answer truthfully. "By asking someone basic non-threatening questions, you are able to observe a response baseline. Ask them about the weather, their plans for the weekend, or any that would elicit a normal, comfortable response. When they respond, observe their body language and eye movement—you want to know how they act when they are telling the truth. Do they shift stance? Glance in one direction or the other? Or look you dead in the eye? Make sure you ask enough questions to observe a pattern" says Jantz. A baseline reading on the person is important for you to be able to distinguish their nervous tics and natural body language and tone of voice from changes that may indicate deceit.

---

[37]*Source: psychologytoday.com*

Next, Jantz recommends you "find the hot spot." The "hot spot" is where people become uncomfortable telling the absolute truth, and while different people may have different "liar's tells" (things they do unconsciously or even physiological changes in the body) that indicates that their stress is increased, which often accompanies a lie. "Once you move from neutral territory to the 'lie zone,' you should be able to observe a change in body language, facial expressions, eye movement, and sentence structure. Everyone will give different subconscious clues when telling a lie, which is why it is so important to observe a normal baseline prior to entering the 'lie zone,'" according to Jantz.

Jantz' third tip is one I often share (and in which I strongly believe): "Watch body language." This is easy to do, but what exactly does a liar's body language look like? Jantz believes that "Liars often pull their bodies inward" when lying to make themselves feel smaller and less noticeable. Many people will become squirmy and sometimes conceal their hands to subconsciously hide fidgety fingers. You might also observe shoulder shrugging." It's important to remember that body language can mean different things in different contexts, and it needs to be viewed not only holistically but also in contrast to the baseline body language. As the noted clinical psychologist and researcher Jack Staas often said, "Sometimes arms folded tightly across a person's chests can indicate defensiveness, in other cases it could mean the person is cold, and in still other cases it could be a comfortable way to sit or stand."[38]

It takes more concentration to lie, and this effort is hard to mask. Jantz advises us to "Observe micro-facial expressions. People will often give away a lie in their facial expression, but some of these facial expressions are subtle and difficult to spot.

Some people will change the facial coloration to a slighter (*sic*) shade of pink, others will flare their nostrils slightly, bit their lip (*sic*) perspire slightly, or blink rapidly. Each of these changes signifies an increase in brain activity as lying begins."

---

[38] *Source: Numerous conversations with Jack Stass.*

Another tip that Jantz offers is to: "Listen to tone, cadence, and sentence structures." This is again why having a baseline reading of the person is so important. Jantz reminds us that "Often when a person is lying, they will slightly change the tone and cadence of their speech. They might start speaking more quickly or slowly and with either a higher or lower tone. Often, the sentences they use become more complex as their brain works on overdrive to keep up with their tale."

And finally, Janz offers this tip on the subject of lying, "watch for when they stop talking about themselves."

People who are lying will also sometimes start removing themselves from their story, and start directing the focus on other people. You will hear fewer "Me's" and "I's" and as liars try to psychologically distance themselves from the lie that they're weaving."

Perhaps most important in Jantz's advice is his one caveat: "Remember: everyone has different lying behavior so there is no one guaranteed lie-detection method. It's most important to be able to compare a liar's baseline behavior to the body movement, facial expressions, eye movement, and verbal cues that they use when they are telling a lie."[39]

Even if you aren't a big fan of psychology, the physiological responses a candidate unconsciously exhibits while lying are worth considering. Since physiological responses happen without the person consciously deciding to behave in this way, they are difficult to fake. In her March 2009 WebMD article "10 Ways to Catch A Liar," Heather Hatfield cites top experts in lie detection that largely echo Jantz's observations. Hatfield starts with a tip from J.J. Newberry, a federal agent "skilled in the art of deception detection." Hatfield tells the story Newberry unraveling a witness's attempt at deception by his recognition of "tell tales (*sic*) signs that a person isn't being honest like inconsistencies in a story, behavior that's different from a person's norm, or too much detail in an explanation" (by the way if you buy that last one, everything I say

---

[39]Source:https://www.psychologytoday.com/us/blog/hope-relationships/201507/6-ways-detect-liar-in-just-seconds

is a lie; I am a compulsive explainer and am continuously providing plodding, painstaking details that are of interest only to me.)

Hatfield takes pains to remind us that it takes years of training to reach the expertise of J.J. Newberry, however, despite this she does offer useful tips for detecting deceptions. "Look for inconsistencies."[40] Judge Judy[41] (for those of you who have been living under a rock for the last ten years or so) is a show where retired family court judge Judith Sheindlin metes out justice to dimwits seriously too stupid watch her show before appearing before her. She yells at people, she calls them stupid, and even offered to explain to one unfortunate "why you're an idiot." Judge Judy is a human lie detector and one of her favorite things to do is to find inconsistencies in people's testimony. She'll say things like "that's not what you told me a moment ago" or" that's not what you said in your sworn complaint" (or answer.) Being called on their inconsistencies seems to trigger other liar's tells so obvious I can spot them as lying dung heaps. Judge Judy is also fond of saying that "if something doesn't make sense then it isn't true."

Another thing that Judge Judy does to expose a liar is to ask seemingly unrelated questions; in a job interview, questions are usually arranged in a logical hierarchy—basic small talk, followed by questions organized around the resumé, questions about work history, etc. But, if you want to find out if the person is a liar, mix up that order and ask something out of the blue to trip up the person. That, I believe, is what Judge Judy is doing. This tactic may seem ridiculous, but remember we want to sort out the liars and violent potential attackers from good candidates who will generally do their best to stay on track and be honest; it may feel like a dirty pool, but then doesn't the liar deserve it?

You can also throw a liar off his or her game by paraphrasing what he or she has told you and questioning things that don't fit with the

---

[40]*I didn't need this article to tell me THAT. I watch Judge Judy daily and you'd better pray that you don't come knocking on my door when I am watching my stories; seriously I will mess you UP.*

[41]*A retooled version of the show, "Judy Justice" is now available on streaming services. I like it better than the original (which I loved.)*

overall lie. Now this may seem redundant with inconsistencies, but the difference is that an inconsistency is just that: a fact the person has asserted as truth that is indisputably at odds with a previous statement the candidate made, but questioning the details of the story relies more on your inferences than on stated assertions. For example, I once had a woman show up 55 minutes late for a job interview. She came into my office and promptly plopped a 64-ounce "Big Gulp" cup filled to the brim with soda. I asked her why she was late and she immediately and adeptly concocted a fable that would make Aesop himself weep in envy. She told an elaborate tale of a horrific highway crash that closed all lanes of the highway (which, incidentally, was visible from our Human Resources lobby window) in painstaking detail—giving minute details and finally finished with a melodramatic, "I got here as soon as I can, my cellphone was dead and I couldn't even get off the highway to call!"

I paraphrased her story back to her and ended with, "What I am a bit unclear about is how you managed to stop at a convenience store and buy that soda, but couldn't stop to call me." Her story fell apart as she sputtered more nonsense about the one pay phone that was available was out of order, and more and more ridiculous details that dug the hole she was in ever deeper. As much as I tried to get past it, I just couldn't shake the feeling that she was a compulsive liar. All the dumbass had to do was leave her soda in the car, but she lacked the foresight and judgment to even do this.

Speaking of compulsive liars, my daughter once told me that I wouldn't have to preface my conversations with "this is a true story" if I didn't lie so much But then again, if I DID lie less frequently, think of how much less you could learn about lying from me; scary isn't it?

Have you ever lied to someone that was interviewing you for a position? If you did, you are far from alone. If you are like most people ,you have, and if you're telling yourself you never have you are probably lying right now (albeit to yourself you sociopathic bastard.) According to a study, on UK job seekers found that half the applicants admitted to lying on their CV and a staggering 75%

felt that it was their bosses' responsibility to uncover the lie. An astonishing 91% said that their bosses never found out.[42]

I get it. I routinely tell people interviewing me that I used to be the U.S. Ambassador to Grease (that's not a typo.) If confronted, I claimed that I was the ambassador to an off-Broadway production of the play and not the country. It was impossible to disprove my deception and may have been the perfect lie.

The fact of the matter is that people will say most anything to get that coveted job offer, and what's more, many more will lie on their resumé, and still more will lie on social media—hell, my Facebook page says I graduated from Harvard (I graduated from the University of Michigan- Dearborn, considered by many to be the Harvard of Dearborn.) And that I work as an Evangelist at the digital Bible. If you can't lie to your friends that you don't care enough about to call on the phone, then seriously who CAN you lie to?

As I researched my first book on the topic, *Lone Gunman: Rewriting the Handbook on Workforce Violence Prevention,* I became interested in what are the most common lies told by people during job interviews (not counting the filthy, filthy lies told by recruiters and hiring managers as they try to woo you.) I came across this gem, "The 10 Most Common Lies That Job Candidates Will Tell You" by Mark Wilkenson.[43] This article is an invaluable resource for constructing questions that you know people are likely to lie about and therefore are useful for identifying how people behave when they are lying. Remember, by asking baseline questions followed by questions that almost all applicants lie about, you will get a feeling for those micro expressions that last but a fraction of a moment but are incredibly strong predictors of deception. So what does Mark Wilkinson assert as the most common lies?

---

[43]*Source: https://www.coburgbanks.co.uk/blog/assessing-applicants/10-common-;oes-job-candidates-tell/*
[44]*Source: I have no idea where I read it, if you MUST have the source then do an internet search you pedantic turd.*

1. **Employment Dates.** I can understand why people want to cover up gaps in employment (many people are laid off for short periods of time, quit before finding another job, or just plain leave a toxic work environment,) but to the intern (or these days, more commonly, the computer algorithm) reading the resume, it looks like the candidate spent a month at Burning Man smoking hash with Gary Busey. This is completely unfair, because even Gary Busey couldn't smoke THAT much hash and even if he could, where would he get enough time to party with all those people? The truth is many, perhaps most, people have gaps in employment that are easily explained, but the resumés are disqualified before they have an opportunity to explain. I read recently that the practice of using algorithms or unqualified personnel to vet resumés is causing many companies to lose strong and desirable candidates and they are shifting back to having more senior hiring professionals vet the resumés, but I suspect that has much more to do with the labor shortage resulting from the Great Resignation than any great epiphany by businesses.

   So, according to Wilkinson, "Those who have gaps that aren't easy to explain (read: locked up abroad) are left with two choices: trying to tell the truth in a more appealing way on their CV and possibly not even getting a call back for jobs or risk it, lie, and hope for the best."

2. **Education.** According to Wilkinson, the second most common lie is a person's education. This is a lie that I know firsthand is shockingly common. Years ago when I had just transitioned from working the assembly line to a white-collar position, after being encouraged to explore other career opportunities along with 60,000 other displaced autoworkers, I found myself getting desperate. The corporate university that I was tasked with creating was sort of a "hurry-up-and-wait" assignment so my boss, the Vice President of Human Resources, asked me to help out by conducting background checks on

candidates in the later portion of the selection process. In my unscientific, statistically invalid research, I found that about 30% of the people lied about their education. Of that, I found about 10% claimed to have earned Master's degrees when they did not, another 70% attended the school listed on their resumés but never finished their degrees, and 10% never attended the school at all.

3. **Skills.** Wilkinson cites lying about one's skills as the third most common lie, in fact, he states that "57% of job candidates embellish their skill set to help them get a job. That's pretty outrageous isn't it?"[45] he asks, I assume rhetorically but I will answer it anyway. I don't know if I would call that outrageous. I speak four languages (five if you count profanity.) The languages are, in order of fluency: English, Spanish, French, and Hungarian (I will leave it to you to figure out where profanity falls on that continuum.) I always thought that I spoke the languages fairly well, until I went to a job interview where one of the two executives interviewing me greeted me in Hungarian and asked me about my flight. I recognized the language as Hungarian and knew precisely what he said to me. I stammered a bit (I hadn't spoken the language regularly for over a decade) and finally admitted to him that I'd guessed my fluency in Hungarian was more than just a bit rusty. He gave me a warm smile (I think won over by my truthfulness) and told me that he had lived for several years in Hungary and worked there as head of the firm's Hungarian office. We talked congenially about the work I had done in Hungary and I was amazed that my gaffe had turned around in my favor. So was I lying about my skills? Was I puffing up or exaggerating my skills? I didn't think so at the time and I don't think so now—I just over estimated my skill level, not in any attempt to deceive (it's not like I was applying as a Hungarian translator or that any of the job requirements would necessitate a fluency in Hungarian; it was just that I was out of practice and I

---

[45] *His words not mine. For all I know he's lying, after all, 63% of all statistics are made up.*

admitted it.) I don't think I was exaggerating, but clearly my claim that I spoke "conversational Hungarian" was no longer true. I speak enough Hungarian to get by, but if I were to return there I would take at least a six-week course in the language. I would say that in my opinion, the more technical the skill, the less likely the candidate is to lie about his or her proficiency in said skill, but I can't because I know some adults who have lied about being proficient in complex and dangerous equipment that they had never even heard of before applying for a position that requires mastery of said equipment. I once interviewed a candidate for a position of an instructional developer. He had claimed on his resumé that he had experience in developing technology-based courses, an area that, while not a job requirement, was a skill set which would be very useful for the position I asked him to tell me about it and he went on to describe a "training course" that he had developed for Excel. I was suitably impressed—after all, this was a subject matter that had a substantial skill set that needed to be mastered.

I asked him what language he programmed it in and he told me English. Thinking he was nervous and had misunderstood my question, I rephrased it and asked him in what computer programming language he had programmed the course. He looked at me blankly, so I asked him a couple of questions and finally asked him if he had written a computer-based program or a job aid (a simple reminder for basic tasks.) Again he stared at me blankly for an uncomfortable amount of time before confessing that he "guessed [he] didn't know the difference." He wasn't malicious, he was (and probably still is) a dope. When I asked him what questions he had for me, he asked, "what would happen if I just didn't show up?" I was confused and beginning to think I might be the butt of a practical joke. I sought clarification. "Do you mean what would happen if you had an emergency and were unable to call in?" He in all earnestness said, "No, I mean what if I just don't feel like coming to work and I just don't show up?" I explained our "no call/no show policy" to him and hastily did my best to usher him out the door. This guy was, is, and forever shall be an imbecile. Whoever helped him falsify his resumé did him no favors. So lying about your skills may not be true dishonesty—it could be exaggeration, overconfidence, a misunderstanding of the nomenclature used to describe the skill, or just out-and-out-stupidity.

4. **Salary.** Wilkenson asserts that the next most common lie is salary (and I don't mean people typically reduce the salary.) While it is true that people feel pressured into inflating their salary, I have to ask, is it really a lie? In many cases people tend to think of their salary as the amount of money they are paid for their employment, but many others think of sala ry as affixed compensation paid to a person in remuneration for services rendered. Let me cut to the quick: if you are asking me how much money I get paid, that is a figure I can give you with great specificity and accuracy. But if you were to ask me how much I am compensated for my employment, I have to consider many benefits to which the exact cost is unknown to me. So I am not about to call someone a liar simply because they have given me a figure that is above—even substantially above—one's base wage.

5. **Weaknesses.** Wilkinsons' next category of lies is weaknesses. Asking the candidate about his or her weaknesses is probably the best way to get an accurate read on the micro-expressions, or liar's tells. When I read this, I immediately thought of Homer Simpson in an episode of The Simpsons where Homer is interviewed for his job at the nuclear plant. Homer, having gotten Marge pregnant with Bart, had to get a grown up job. The nuclear plant was hiring, so he applied. Smithers, the assistant to the plant owner, is conducting the interviews and since there are only three candidates for two jobs, he decides to interview the candidates simultaneously. Smithers asks the question, "What is your greatest weakness?" The first candidate

quickly and confidently fires back that he drives himself too hard. The second candidate, with equal enthusiasm and vigor, says that he's a bit of a perfectionist. And then Homer slowly and awkwardly says "Well, it takes me a long time to learn anything. I'm kind of a goof-off...a little stuff starts disappearing from the workplace...,"" to which an incredulous Smithers says, "That's enough!"

The scene is comic because if you asked someone to describe weakness, like as not, you will get one of the first two answers given by Homer's competition. The intended audience for Wilkinson's article is made up of recruiters, and while Wilkinson weakly suggests that the recruiter could ask a tougher question like, "Yes, but that's not really not a weakness is it? Could you give me another answer?" Wilkinson doesn't see much value in the question and outside the context of determining deception and liar's tells, he is probably right. But do we want to provoke the candidate into a snotty, condescending, or aggressive response? Then the question becomes invaluable to us.

Who would you hire? The person who responds with a sarcastic, "Well I'm beginning to think answering stupid quesions is one of my weaknesses," or gives no response whatsoever? Or the person who provides a pleasant and polite "I'm sorry, but I really can't think of any right now; my performance reviews have all been exemplary. I acknowledge that there are areas in which I can improve, but none are coming to mind at the moment," or " I know I've given you a standard answer, and one that you probably have heard often, but could we maybe focus on the areas where I think I have the greatest opportunity to learn, or perhaps frame the question in some other, more positive way?" The first response may denote an ill-tempered jerk who can't even manage to hold it together long enough to get through an interview. The second response (no response) exposes someone who is either too non-assertive to speak up (and therefore a potential target.) The final answers are typical of someone who is assertive and self-confident. I have used the technique to turn a question on its ear—demonstrating that I knew the intent of the question, but preferred to put a more positive spin on the subject (and thus indicating that I tended to focus on positive opportunities rather than on negativity) without being deceptive or contrary. I did have one HR generalist bristle at my response and I didn't get the job because the generalist didn't know his rectum from a jelly donut.

I am not going to go through all of Wilkinson's lies, but there is one more I think is worth addressing: references.

6. **References.** Whether or not someone is lying about a reference isn't as important as the judgment or lack of judgment the candidate has shown in selecting his or her references. You could certainly question the value of checking someone's references. I mean, only a person with the judgment of a syphilitic baboon would knowingly provide references who are likely to give anything other than a stellar review. But when it comes to references, the lie tends to be a BIG lie and the candidate has given you a perfect source for verifying the truthfulness of the statements they have already made during the interview or on his or her resumé.

When it comes to references, many people will fudge the relationship they have with the reference and instead of providing business contacts (as typically asked) will provide the names of family, friends, or neighbors. LinkedIn (before it became a lame piece of crap where idiots post inane polls and every other post is an advertisement) added a new element to this. I now receive about three requests a month for recommendations (on their profile) from people I have never met, apart from being connected (if someone is a fan of my work my ego will not allow me to turn down their invitation to connect) on the site. For all I know, they could live with a blow-up doll that they have so badly abused that it can only talk about it in a therapist's office using, I assume, smaller dolls. And people, myself included, will ask people to be their reference without really knowing what questions will be asked or how the references will answer the questions put to them.

One of my references, a person with whom I had worked for almost a decade at two different companies, responded to a question about my greatest weakness by saying, "Sometimes Phil gets impatient with people who don't see his genius soon enough."[46] Of all the weaknesses he could have chosen, and they are legion and the things of prurient legends, he chose this one. It worked. It got me the job, but the dullards who hired me were surprised that I am INDEED impatient with the mouth-breathing dolts indifference to my genius. Why ask a question if you are going to ignore the answer?

My favorite story about lying about references on a job application is from the Mary Tyler Moore Show: when the perpetually clueless News Anchor, Ted Baxter, used Jacques Cousteau as a reference because he reasoned Cousteau would be impossible to get ahold of. That makes a lot of sense to me.

Don't Over-Rely On Lies

Sometimes I inadvertently repeat myself. Other times, I deliberately repeat myself multiple times to drive home a point. Lying is just one red flag, albeit an important one, but even so our goal should be to get a broader picture of who the candidate is, not just when they are putting their "interview face" on. I have an acquaintance who is excellent at getting jobs and most particularly he is adept at interviewing. He gets hired a lot and then quits (at least according to him) because he has an incredibly abysmal work ethic; point being a candidate is putting his or her best foot forward in an interview, and sadly too many people worry (to an incredible extent) about getting a job and give virtually no thought to whether or not they are a good fit for it. Good interviewing skills aren't the same as good skills in other areas. But that's not why I am cautioning against putting too much faith in deception detection.

---

[46]*His assessment was completely accurate—I hate it when people don't immediately recognize my genius, but I wish he would have let my new employer discover that on its own.*

When Is The Truth Really A Lie And Vice Versa

When I was discharged from my position as a Mutilation Controller at General Motors, I was laid off from my employer but was collecting unemployment and supplemental pay. I still retained my benefits, and was still on the company roll as an employee. This continued for a year, with the only difference being that I didn't go to the factory and work. So by most measures I was still an employee, at least in my mind and in the minds of the United Auto Workers (UAW) and General Motors. So whenever I gave my work history to potential employers, I never felt like I was telling the entire truth but at the same time I didn't feel I was being deceptive. Even so, someone else could read my resumé and assume that I had lied about my length of employment and in the end make some grievous erroneous conclusions about my character. At any rate, I default to the date I was hired until the day I was laid off, even if it makes my tenure look far shorter than what it was. In fact, while I wasn't expected to report to the plant during the layoff, I was still as far as the company was concerned still employed, but inactive. So in effect I

Planning Your Interview

In today's business climate, a well executed interview can literally mean the difference between life and death. I know that sounds melodramatic, but I don't care—you wouldn't just go through the motions when choosing a heart surgeon, and you shouldn't just hire a construction contractor without verifying that the contractor is licensed, insured, and above all able to do the job. So I ask you, is hiring someone to join your workforce without ensuring that they don't have a history of violence or other factors that may predispose them to violence? There are good ways to interview job candidates and bad ways, and there is plenty of information about how to conduct a good interview readily available on-line, but scarce few of them are written through the lens of workplace violence prevention.

A friend of mine who has owned his owned business (since he agreed to work for a friend for free for three years in exchange for an equity stake in the company when he was in his twenties and parlayed the sizeable sum of money he made from this decision into a series of profitable small businesses) recently told me, "we have a zero crazy policy in our hiring." I asked what he meant and he said, "I have 6-8 people interview each candidate and if any one of them, and I mean any individual, gets a creepy vibe from a candidate they are no longer considered." This interview structure may be time-consuming and you may risk losing a good candidate, but you won't end up (at least in theory) hiring a rampage killer.

A good interview begins with a plan, and as much as people THINK that they can just wing it when it

comes to interviewing, there are numerous reasons why that is a less than smart idea. Your interview plan should answer the questions of "who," "what," "why," "where," "when," and "how."

Who?

Obviously one answer to the "who" in your plan is the candidate(s), but you also should know well in advance who on your staff will be interviewing each candidate. There is no set rule as to who should be included and who should not, but I have found that a group interview saves time and more importantly adds an element of stress to the interview that increases the odds that an unstable or otherwise undesirable candidate will reveal him or herself. A team interview also affords the people who are not asking questions at the moment time to more carefully observe changes in body language, posture, or other tells. Another advantage of a team interview is that as the interviewers take turns asking questions, they can ask the same question another team member has asked but phrased just a bit differently and listen for consistency. It is important that each candidate get asked a standard set of questions, but they need not be asked by the same team members; this is crucial to avoid any perception of illegal discrimination.

What?

Each question should be carefully crafted in advance of the interview and each team member should know these questions by heart. But even more than this, everyone involved in conducting the interview should be cognizant of exactly what insights can be gleaned by the candidate's answers to the questions.

When you plan your interviews your questions should fall in one of four categories: baseline questions, "hot spot" questions, integrity questions, and job suitability questions. I will explain each of these categories in a moment.

Where?

The pandemic, labor shortage, and work-from-home have put HR professionals and hiring managers at a grave disadvantage when it comes to interviewing. Not long ago interviews were conducted at the company, typically in a conference room or an office. In those contexts it was relatively easy to get a lot of information very quickly from a candidate before he or she even spoke. Experts disagree on the exact percentage of communication that is nonverbal, but then experts disagree on everything up to and including the existence of BigFoot, whether or not the greatest scientific minds in the galaxy slough just over four light years to do anal probes on two drunken buffoons who got lost in a swamp, and precisely what constitutes an "expert." The experts cannot even consistently differentiate between oral communication and verbal communication. "Oral" means using one's mouth, while "verbal" means using words. This means that if you are communicating in writing (unless you are using pictograms) you are communicating verbally. Similarly, unless you are using interpretive dance to communicate your point you are communicating verbally. One thing on which the experts in nonverbal communication *can* agree is that the majority of communication is nonverbal. I can attest to this—I have traveled extensively and while I speak (at various proficiency) a smattering of English, Spanish, Hungarian, and French, I have also traveled to countries where the language sounded to me like inscrutable gibberish. I relied on what Native Americans described as "hand talk." Hand talk was a series of motions and gestures used either to augment a point or to replace verbal language altogether. When I travel, I look and feel like a Cheyenne brave giving directions to hapless travelers looking to make that big score in California. I may look a tad undignified, but it works.

Nonverbal communication can be tone of voice, gestures, posture, facial expressions; none of which are likely to completely come through in a phone interview or a virtual meeting. So whenever possible, meet the candidate in person. I had one company fly me from Detroit to Chicago for a lunch interview and I must say, I felt that the company was very serious about me and the importance of the position for which I was being considered. This is not to say that a round of phone screening isn't appropriate; it is, but never accept a phone or virtual interview as a substitute for an in-person interview. There is too much at stake, and hiring the wrong person could end in bloodshed and tragedy.

In negotiations, many believe that having the negotiations on your turf is the best way to win, but in this case I disagree with that approach. I prefer to conduct interviews in a conference room or over a meal than in an office. Why? Because your office provides a myriad of clues about who you are and what is important to you, making it very easy for a liar to deduce exactly what you want to hear and tell it to you. Interviewing over a meal is an excellent way to relax a candidate and to mess up the candidate's script. Once the candidate is off-script, it is more likely that something revealing of their character will slip out—positively or negatively.

When?

I am always surprised when a recruiter or hiring manager suggests that we meet for a job interview in the middle of a workday. My typical response is to suggest that we meet before or after work or during my lunch break. I view interviewing for a new position on company time a form of theft—the company is not paying me to interview for another job, and frankly I don't want to take a vacation day to be interviewed. I am very open about my objection to the interview during the work day and I am surprised at the positive response when I tell the prospective employer, "I would prefer that we meet at a time when I am not being paid to look for another job. I am paid to do my current job. Just as I would never cheat you out of wages, I don't feel comfortable cheating my current employer." If, however, I do decide to take the day off work, I will make it clear to the recruiter that I am sacrificing a personal day, and if possible, I would like to schedule multiple interviews in the same day.

Why?

Every interview question must have a reason for the interviewer to ask it. I was once asked by an obviously poor interviewer whether I had a Napoleon complex. I was nonplussed and answered honestly. I told him that I am 5'7" and that according to the most recent data, 5'9" is the average height for American males. I never considered myself short. I told him that I knew plenty of people who were taller than me and plenty that were shorter than me, and so I never gave much thought of my height. I don't think the interviewer was trying to provoke me and while this question could really be useful in determining whether someone had a propensity for violence, the rest of his questions seemed muddled and some of them didn't even make sense. I didn't take the job. Obviously he didn't ask every candidate this question (unless he was only interviewing diminutive men) and there were other tells that made me think that this guy was not someone for whom I wanted to work. But the question of "why" goes much deeper than merely asking yourself "why should I hire this person?" but also "why do you want to work here?" If we are being truly honest the answer is probably either, "because I need a job" or "because this job pays more" or so forth. But what we really need to understand is "why did you apply for THIS particular job at THIS particular company?" These questions will help us to determine if this person wants to work for us for the right reasons and thus be a better fit.

How?

In the context of preventing violence, every question should have a darned good and clear reason for being asked and everyone on the team should be crystal clear on why the question is being asked. As you plan your questions, ask yourself what is your objective in asking it. To some extent this goes to the "why?" of an interview, but in this case *how* you ask the question is more about phrasing, tone of voice, posture, and other nonverbal cues that you are giving to the candidate.

Baseline questions:

Baseline questions are questions that are innocuous and only pathological liars would bother to lie about them. When asking baseline questions (and much of this has been covered in the section on identifying deceptive responses, but is important enough to warrant repeating) you should be carefully observing the subject's body language, mannerisms, and micro-expressions so that you will be able to detect changes in these when the candidate starts lying like their pants are on fire. Some good baseline questions include:

Question: How do you like this weather?

Why It's A Good Question: A neutral question like this puts the person at ease allowing the interviewer to get a sense of his or her mannerisms and nonverbal messaging.

Question: Did you have any trouble finding us?

Why It's A Good Question: Again, this question is innocuous and usually interpreted as friendly small talk. Be careful when you analyze candidates' responses to this question, however, because the candidate may be so into "interview mode" that they may actually interpret this question as a test of his or her ability to follow directions and lie about the difficulty that they had finding your location.

Keep your questions neutral—no talk of politics, sports, or anything controversial: just keep it light and stick to topics of conversation you might have while waiting in line for a bus.

Hotspot Questions

Hotspot questions are the questions that most people will answer with a lie. By carefully observing the changes in the candidate's posture, facial expressions, tone of voice, eye contact, and other nonverbal cues and by comparing these cues to those you observed during the baseline questions, you can gain a strong indication of when the answer to one of your questions is an attempt to deceive you. Here are some good examples of hotspot questions:

Question: Describe a situation where you were fired or laid off (note: if the person says that they have never been fired or laid off—many people have not—then ask them to instead describe a situation where they were reprimanded.)

Why It's A Good Question: Even if this person has never been fired, he or she will likely react to the question. In this case, the fewer the details the candidate provides the more likely it is that the person is telling the truth and being completely honest. For example, if the respondent says, "I've never been fired, but I was laid off; it made me unhappy," then it is likely a more truthful answer than, "I wasn't actually fired, but there was an instance where my coworker was stealing and the boss accused the entire night shift of stealing $34 out of the till. Many of us told the boss that it was unfair to accuse everyone for something that might even have been an honest mistake. We were all accused of being disrespectful, and I quit. It was only later that I found out the entire night shift was fired." The former answers the question directly and without excess emotion or details (nobody wants to provide a lot of detail about a situation that was unpleasant.) The latter, by contrast, provides a rich tapestry of details that are neither necessary nor all that entertaining; furthermore the respondent is quick to start talking about the other people involved as if he or she was an observer and not a participant. When a person starts providing too much detail, or becomes evasive, you should watch this person carefully as he or she will likely be giving away all their liar's tells.

Question: Do you have any reason to believe that you could be targeted for violence?

Why It's A Good Question: There is nothing quite like cutting to the quick (no sick pun intended) when asking about the possibility of workplace violence. Personally my notoriety is such that I have numerous enemies. Because of my outspoken views on the shortcomings of the field of safety and my refusal to call a turd a Baby Ruth bar just to soothe the egos of those who either cling to outmoded, dimwitted, safety folklore, or threaten (through my criticism) the livelihoods of the shysters who shill feces and call it chocolate icecream, I have received death threats, a bomb threat, and numerous threats of violence—but let me just say two things: 1) only an idiot tells you that he or she is going to kill you BEFORE he (it's usually men who are bomb builders) are actually in the act and, 2) I honestly believe that you aren't saying anything anyone needs to hear if you don't rile people up. Nobody has ever asked me in a job interview if I had any reason to believe that I could be targeted for violence I would have to say "yes."If the person seems uncomfortable, hesitates, or takes a long time carefully choosing his or her words, it could indicate that he or she believes that he or she might well be targeted for violence and is either uncomfortable answering truthfully or desperately trying to make a statement that is technically true but still deceptive. But let's be realistic here; when we are interviewing we are putting our best foot forward and when one is a victim or a target of violence he or she may blame his or her self—it's not exactly something that most people would showcase. I cannot emphasize enough how wrong it is to discriminate against targets of violence. With this having been said, you should take extra precautions to protect the targets of violence and his or her coworkers[47]

Integrity Questions

Integrity questions are designed to provide insights into the character of the candidate. Obviously, you will want to have a good idea of liars' tells when asking these questions. In this case, the WAY in which the person answers the question is far more important than the answer itself (with some obvious exceptions.) Some good questions for ascertaining a person's integrity include:

---

[47]*While respecting the new employee's privacy*

Question: Tell me about a situation where you had a difficulty in a relationship (that could be a personal or professional relationship) where the other person was uncooperative. How did you handle that?

Why It's A Good Question: A truly unstable individual will usually talk about problems with a coworker or a boss, but sometimes a candidate, particularly younger candidates without extensive professional experience, will talk about conflict with a friendship or love interest. As the candidate answers the question, be alert to his or her body language. Does the question make the individual uncomfortable? Does the tone of the individual's voice change and sound aggressive? Does the individual avoid the conflict or talk about a passive-aggressive response? A candidate's body language and tone of voice often can belie either a violent personality or a passive personality; the former is a red flag for obvious reasons and the latter is dangerous because a person who has passive, or passive-aggressive, personality is more likely to be a victim of domestic violence and thus put your organization at a higher risk of becoming a target of a single shooter event. I cannot emphasize this enough: job interviews are not used for the purpose of discriminating against victims of domestic violence, but forewarned is forearmed and if you suspect domestic violence, the compassionate action to take is not to pass over an otherwise qualified candidate, rather to redouble your efforts to explain the measures you have in place to protect workers wherever they are working.

Question: Tell me about the circumstances of the departure from your last employer?

Why It's A Good Question: People tend to rehearse job interviews and are likely to have a pat answer for "why did you leave your last employer?" or "why are you looking to leave your current employer?" By framing the question this way, the applicant is forced to tell you a story, and that story will likely provide you with far more information and far richer details than the repeatedly rehearsed answer. Don't be afraid to ask the applicant follow-up questions like, "describe your relationship with your boss" or "was your boss supportive of your decision to leave?" Or even questions like "what did you like most about your former employer?" or "what did you dislike most about your former employer?" These kinds of probing questions will give you greater insight into the applicant's interpersonal skills. Don't settle for easy answers like "it was a bad fit." Instead, follow up with the question "why was it a bad fit?" or "what makes you think it was a bad fit?"

Question: Tell me about a time when you were involved in an instance of bullying. How did you handle that?

Why It's A Good Question: A candidate may honestly never have encountered a bully in a professional setting, but most of us have been bullied or have bullied someone at some point in our lives. If the candidate avoids the question, for example, they might say, "I don't think I have encountered any bullying," then broaden the question by saying "certainly you must have some experience, perhaps as a child, or where you witnessed a bullying situation; talk to me about that." If the person still claims that they have no experience with bullying, you will have to judge whether or not the person is being truthful or is trying to avoid an uncomfortable answer. Again, here is a situation where the candidate's body language will likely provide key cues as to whether or not they are being truthful.

Question: If a stranger was able to view your social media pages, what conclusions would they likely draw about you?

Why It's A Good Question: Recently, a friend told me that a potential employer asked her to provide her Facebook page. I am not crazy about this practice because asking for it outright seems rude and overly intrusive, and employers need to remember that the recruiting and screening process is as much about the prospect deciding whether or not your organization is a place where they wish to be employed as it is about whether or not you wish to employ a candidate. By asking the candidate what conclusions a stranger might make based on his or her social media presence, you are able to see the person through their own lens, albeit a likely filtered lens. This not only tells you how the individual sees his or herself but also forces the individual to reflect on how the world sees him or her; this can often suss out feelings of persecution or aggression. But remember that not all aggressive posts are serious—I have been in Facebook jail so many times I am thinking of getting tear drop tattoos on my eyes.

Question: How would your former co-workers describe you?

Why It's A Good Question: The response to this question can be very telling— more because of how the applicant reacts than how he or she answers. Does the candidate's body language stiffen or seem defensive? How do the applicant's demeanor and voice change when asked this question? With all this in mind, remember that despite all this introspection, the person whom you are interviewing may be so narcissistic or sociopathic that he or she may not recognize how people truly see him or her. Also, a true sociopath is typically unable to empathize and therefore may answer by saying things akin to "I don't know."

Job Suitability Questions

Job suitability questions are designed to determine if the person can physically, mentally, and emotionally do the job day in and day out and feel fulfilled working in your job environment, and, perhaps more importantly, whether or not you want them working on your team. These questions are as varied as the jobs themselves and you shouldn't have any difficulty constructing these questions. Remember the liars' tells, however—a desperate job seeker may well lie through his or her tobacco stained teeth and misrepresent their aptitude and team spirit with every fetid breath they exhale, but by knowing their tells you can sort the wheat from the chaff and you will be far less likely to hire the wrong person.

Remember to ask all the candidates the SAME questions to avoid the appearance of (or even presence of) illegal bias. This practice protects people against discrimination for employment for a variety of reasons that the candidate cannot control. One of the easiest tests to PROVE illegal discrimination is to show a pattern of asking one group of people more questions, or more probing questions, or…well you get the picture.

This list is far from all-inclusive and remember the whole point of the interview isn't just to find a qualified candidate, but also to find a good—and *relatively* safe—addition to your team.

Summary

Interviews are an essential way to weed out the weirdos, but the law protects certain classes of people—usually people against who have traditionally been discriminated against—but that doesn't include people with a propensity for violence. Social media posts of a candidate can provide you insight not just into people's personal habits but also, to a large extent, their judgment.

When interviewing someone it is intensely important that you have at least a cursory knowledge of liars' tells; those subconscious and nonverbal cues that tell you when someone is lying.

There are four categories of questions one should ask during a job interview: baseline, hot spot, integrity, and job suitability questions. Baseline questions are the questions one asks while making small talk and they are useful in establishing the gestures, facial expressions, posture, and tone of voice when anyone (who is not a sociopath) would most likely not be lying. Hot spot questions are questions one asks to irritate or corner a candidate so one can gauge how nonverbal signals change when they are stressed or lying. Integrity questions are designed to provide insights into the character of the candidate. Integrity questions provide key insights especially if you can read the person's liar's tells. Finally, job suitability questions aren't just about finding out whether or not a candidate is qualified to do the job, but also about how well they fit with the other team members, and most importantly will they find the job enjoyable and fulfilling.

Thought Starters

Have you ever lied during a job interview or screening? Why or why not?

Do you think you would be able to spot a person's liars' tells? Why or why not?

Stop. Don't Shoot!

Chapter 9: The Importance Of A Probationary Period

I have always been wary of recently hired employees who become too relaxed and comfortable in a new work environment too quickly. I am a gregarious, talkative, and (most of the time) friendly guy who is quick to welcome the new employee to the team. Despite this, I have always been put off by the lack of what I call "new-employee behavior." Whenever a person starts a new position, the new employee tends to tread lightly while exploring the corporate norms, boundaries, and written policies (versus the practiced policies.) In short, new employees try to ease their angst by trying to conform to the cultural norms. Whenever I see a new employee who swaggers through the workplace, I get a sick feeling in the pit of my stomach; the lack of new-hire behavior makes me wonder at the limits of a person like that. If the new hire is acting overly confident and socially inappropriate NOW, then what can we expect of that person when he or she gets truly comfortable?

Years ago I worked with a tight-knit group of consultants on a revolutionary and innovative culture change initiative for a large international manufacturer. At first we were hired simply to review proposals submitted by machine tool builders to provide training. Most of the companies had never been asked to provide training and few, if any, knew how to go about such an undertaking. When I was hired I was floundering in a position as Head of Training (for which I was hired literally a month before I started my first class in the University's Training, Design, and Development certificate program) and three months in I was deeply in over my head. I was in a suit and tie workplace and my previous experience had been on a factory floor. Forget not knowing how to run a training department, I didn't even know how to behave in a white collar world. Fortunately, I had a mentor who told me, "I can't teach you how to be a trainer, but I can teach you how to behave and be successful in an office environment." He did, and I learned quickly—many tips that I still use too many decades later. But I didn't know how to deliver the technical demands people were making—I had made the rookie mistake of worrying so much about getting the job that I didn't worry enough about if I could be successful DOING the job. Simultaneously I was sinking in debt and my marriage was failing. Then, to make matters worse, a woman who worked in Marketing decided that she wanted my job. She had no experience but was well liked, and threatened to quit if she wasn't given my job. It was a shitty thing for her to do, but my boss had been promoted to another department and I didn't stand a chance. Things were looking pretty grim. Just when things looked their worst, the phone rang. On the other end was the head of my department from the university. He told me that he had a job for me. I explained to him that I couldn't do the job I had at the time, but he reassured me by telling me that they would teach me everything I needed. It was the first time I was interviewed by four people at once, but I aced it. Unbeknownst to me, one of the people who interviewed me was in my college cohort. He and the other guy who did the same job welcomed me and showed me the ropes. I was (and those of you who know me or have read my other works will find this hard to believe) a model employee and a quick study. It wasn't long before I was developing training programs like a veteran, and yes, for the first 90 days or so I was strictly acting like "the new guy." As my tenure grew, so did the tight relationship with my team. We worked hard but also managed to have fun. Lunch was a standing date and it wasn't long before I felt completely comfortable joking around with the team and grinding out the mountain of work ahead of us. Then one day the chief consultant, who I still refer to as the Devil, hired a fresh new team member.[48] The fact that no one who actually did the job got to interview him rubbed most of us the wrong way, but I decided to give him a chance. The plant was on a two week "shut down," which meant that almost no one besides our team was working.

Chett, the new guy, was acting peculiar from day one. I was listening to my music when he turned to me and said, "turn that crap off; it's horrible." I told him that if he didn't like it there were more appropriate ways to ask me to lower the volume, and that I was not going to turn it off because my other teammates were also enjoying it. He went on a tirade about how stupid I was for listening to the music and insulting me for a lack of musical taste. One of my teammates came to my defense and told him that it would be best to let it go. He did, but got little digs in for the next couple of days. On day two, he offered to drive to lunch and when we got into his car we found multiple pornographic magazines (for the record I am no prude, but this was so hard core that it made me wince.) The head of the project was horrified, but Chet just waved her off, dismissing her outrage as being "too sensitive." On day three he bragged about how much he was making. It was twice what the highest paid person on the team was making. It didn't bother me because I knew that after the pornography incident, he wouldn't last long. The next day, he changed the name tag (using white out) of a colleague from "Haulter" to "Haulterstein." When the project leader saw it she looked stricken; I guess we all must have. "What's the matter?" Chett stammered, "Is he Jewish?" He was. Chett, in less than a single week, lost his dream job. I wonder about him from time to time, mostly about whether he learned his lesson or went on to become a corporate nightmare.

---

[48]*While I was an independent consultant, and hence my own boss, I did work as part of a team of consultants.*

In another case (at another company,) a coworker came to me with the résumé of a person being considered for an open position. I looked at the document and remarked that the individual had six jobs in two years and I found that disquieting. My coworker told me that she had had the same initial response, but that she had interviewed him and he had a good answer for his short tenure at each of his jobs. I then interviewed him, but immediately caught a bad vibe from him and told her about my misgivings using specific, observable examples of why I thought he would be a bad hire. For example, he had spent several tours in the military but left abruptly one year shy of qualifying for a pension. When I asked him about it, he told me that he didn't want to talk about it and left me questioning his judgment. I thought it was suspicious and indicative of extremely poor judgment (coupled with his gruff "I don't want to talk about that" response) but thought, "Who am I to make (or pass) judgments on another person's life choices?"

When I voiced my concerns to my coworker, she dismissed them outright and accused me of not wanting to hire another man who would challenge my "alpha dog" status. I found the accusation insulting and told her so, adding, "Hey, he will be your employee so if things go south, it's your problem."

Soon the president of the company came to me and asked me to come to his office to talk. He told me that hiring this man shouldn't be perceived as a threat to me, and that I will always have a position of leadership and expertise in the organization. I explained to him that I was asked for my opinion and gave it. I told him that I was not threatened but: 1) the man was far from 100% qualified to do the job (I estimated he was maybe 35% qualified,) 2) he would require extensive training that would fall to me and I wasn't sure how well that would sit with him, and 3) his job history over the past two years showed that he had an average tenure of three months on the job, and had gaps between each indicating, to me at least, a strong possibility of abrupt dismissals and/or quitting.

They hired him and he was almost immediately a problem. I don't remember what set him off, but he came into my office shouting at me about some perceived grievance and he even hinted that he might be provoked into violence. I went to his manager and to the president of the company and reported the incident and predictably, they did nothing except dismiss my complaints, telling me "you're just looking to find fault," and "you never liked him and nothing he does will ever please you." As a point of fact, I did like him when he wasn't throwing tantrums.

Over the next couple of months there were other indicators that this man was a hot-head and potentially unstable. He complained bitterly about his neighbors with whom he was feuding (not a neighbor, but multiple neighbors.) I knew how his manager and the president would respond to my concerns so I said nothing.

On several occasions this guy would go off his nut and send me long, rambling emails containing threats both veiled and overt. In one, a 5-page missive, he told me we could handle a situation in one of two ways: "hard or easy." In each case, I printed out the emails and put them in a file folder that I kept in my desk drawer. In each case, I said nothing.

One day his manager came into my office, closing my door and locking it behind her as she entered. She was visibly shaken as she handed me several printed pages. She had received an email similar to the ones I was now routinely getting. I read it and pulled out the thick file from the desk drawer. She read a couple and left, but moments later pulled me into an impromptu meeting with the president of the company, where I was asked why I had not come forward with my emails sooner. I told them flat out that it was because: A) I didn't believe that they would believe me, and B) Even if they did believe me, they would take no action. The individual was fired soon after the meeting.

At this point the manager was terrified that he would come and shoot up the office and the company took appropriate measures to secure the office. "But what about the parking lot?" his manager asked me, and I didn't have an answer. Fortunately, he never returned, and we never heard from him again, but it is safe to say that it wouldn't take many other variables to have this become a rampage killing in our workplace, and one that could have been predicted and prevented.

These two stories illustrate how easy it is to look the other way in the effort to avoid a confrontation. But handling these two bad hires by doing nothing is akin to trying to avoid being run over by a train by closing your eyes and covering your ears as the locomotive comes barrelling down the tracks at you; it's a plan of a sort, it's just a bad one.

It's fine to grouse and complain about bad hires, but complaining about a bad hire doesn't change anything. We all try to avoid bad hires anyway, but in many cases we are so eager to hire someone (especially in a tight labor market) that we convince ourselves that we can somehow fit the square peg into a round hole. What's worse is that when it's obvious that no amount of effort will get that square peg into the round hole, we just live with it or in the worst case, die because of it.

Addressing Problem Probationary Employees

The first and best way to address problem probationary employees is to provide a comprehensive new employee orientation on (or very close to) the employee's first day on the job. While it is important to make it very clear what constitutes acceptable and unacceptable behavior, you don't want it to become a session on 101 Ways to Get Fired. While working at a global automotive supplier it fell to me to develop a new employee orientation. Given my bias against the big book of things that will get you fired, I met with the Vice President of Human Resources and bounced some ideas around with him.

We both agreed that it sends the wrong message to greet a person who you have worked tirelessly and sometimes frantically to hire with "okay, now that you're hired here's why we will fire you." Conversely, the Chief Legal Counsel insisted that the regulations and rules be a part of this effort. Working with a small team, we created the "Employee Owner's Manual" (the executives wanted something "automotive themed.") The final product was nothing like a traditional employee handbook—all the chapters had names like "On-Board Navigation" (describing the corporate structure.) Training was under the heading of "Routine Maintenance." As sickeningly cutesy as all this sounds, it was incredibly effective. Even so, knowing what I now know, I would have done something different: I would have written instructions for the supervisors on how to evaluate not just the work performance of the individual, but also the cultural fit, and ways to weed out those people who through their aberrant and sometimes bizarre behaviors belie a deep and troublesome insight into their potential future behavior. In other words the people that for whatever reason make you shake your head and wonder if this is what they do in week one, what will they do in six months; the weirdos who don't quite give you the creeps, but they give you a feeling that is "creeps adjacent".

Many people will tell you that you should sweep in at the first sign of trouble and implement your company's disciplinary process, but how do you discipline someone for being an oddball who displays behaviors that, for lack of a better description, just feel "wrong" for a new employee?

Here are some simple techniques you can use to weed out the newly hired employees that give you cause to believe that they could be the source of greater problems later:

- **Define the "Probationary Period."** I like to explain that the 90-day probation is like an on-the-job interview for which you are paid. The candidate has told you certain areas in which he or she is proficient and the probationary period is a means to determine whether or not what you were told in the interview is true. In the context of this book we should note that while we are talking about watching for signs that the person is capable of violence, even in cases where violence isn't your primary concern this is still a good standard practice. When explaining just what the probationary period means, be sure to explain in no uncertain terms that the worker's employment can be terminated for no cause (assuming that they are "at-will employees.")

- **Clearly Identify your Expectations.** Expectations of competency, cultural fit (does the person exhibit the values and behaviors expected by the company?) and social interactions with other employees.

- **Observe.** Your observations of a new employee may be key to identifying whether or not a probationary employee transitions to a long-term employee or to the street. While observing the employee, remember to document what you saw, why you felt it was inappropriate, and how you felt about it. Focus more on behaviors than anything else and avoid ascribing what the individual was feeling (attitude.) And whatever you do, don't make excuses for the abnormal behavior.[49]

- **Establish Regular Touch Points**. When you begin the probationary period, establish a set time each week where you can provide the probationary employee information on his or her suitability so far.

- **Look For Atypical Behaviors.** Look for signals that a new employee might be capable of violence (or to a lesser extent, just a bad overall fit.) These signals include:

  o **Temper tantrums.** The only place a temper tantrum should be considered normal (although inappropriate nonetheless) is a daycare center. While it is possible to have a veteran employee who acts like a dysfunctional turd that throws temper tantrums on a routine basis in allowing this behavior these companies are at significant risk of a workplace violence incident because allowing this behavior sends a message that this behavior is appropriate, not just to the person throwing a tantrum, but to other employees as well.[50]

---

[49] *Let's take a minute here to discuss exactly what I mean by the word "normal." Normal refers to thoughts and behaviors that are within the societal, cultural, or organizational standards (i.e., norms.) Within "normal" are outliers—the little quirks that some people have that are different from the rest, like wearing the same color pants every day; this might seem abnormal to some people, but it wouldn't be considered so odd that it would be alarming, while having pornography on one's desk would be outside the norm, provided of course that you don't work in the adult publication business.*

[50] *Yes, believe it or not there are ample examples of companies who allow this behavior to go unchallenged, not just by veterans but by people across the spectrum of previous occupations.*

o **Horseplay.** There are many places where horseplay is tolerated but shouldn't be. The quintessential question as to whether or not a given behavior is appropriate is "is this a part of the reason we pay this employee a wage?" By definition, horseplay is not behavior for which most employers want to pay.

o **Back talk.** Not everyone has the right to boss a new employee around, and the probationary hire may resent the person who tries to offload their tasks thinking that they probably may not know any better. It's completely understandable that the new hire might balk at such an assignment, but there is a chasm of difference between "screw you! That's not my job." and "I'm sorry, but I have to check with my supervisor before taking on any more assignments, can I get back with you tomorrow?"

o **Aggression.** Aggression can manifest itself in several ways—from bossing someone around or shouting to pushing or grabbing someone, or even aggressive posture.

o **Non-Conformity.** I am the altar at which all other nonconformists go to pray. With that said, I have the sense to curb my natural oddball state until I know what conforming looks like in a given environment, including the workplace. The first thing a new member of a group tends to do is to observe the group to learn what is acceptable and what is not. For example, there is no good reason that I should have to wear a shirt to work, and yet I wear one. Some people just aren't bound by convention and sometimes that lack of a willingness can be dangerous. Van Gogh was nonconventional, but then so was Ed Gien, and I don't think I would want to have to deal with their crap day-in day-out.

- **Act quickly.** If a new employee is acting outside the new employee norms, you need to act immediately. The urgency and intensity of your actions should be directly proportionate to the actions of the individual, but it doesn't take much before an action rises to the level where you will need to involve your Human Resources department or Legal Council. Andrew Arena is a partner in a consulting firm that specializes in workplace violence prevention and he says "I always advise business clients to highly encourage all employees to make such orders known to Human Resources (HR) …t can only help if someone is made aware."

- **Provide Feedback.** Feedback is one of the most important and powerful tools at your disposal. Unfortunately, most people know more about killing gophers than they do about effectively giving feedback. Fortunately I have spent a career teaching effective ways of providing others with constructive feedback. Feedback is so important in this context that I have decided to devote an entire subsection to it. Don't try to talk me out of it…my mind's made up and arguing with a book, besides being a bit sanity challenged, will result in your words falling on un-hearing, uncaring, and indifferent ears.

Feedback

The probationary period is especially important both to the newly hired and to the organization. The strongest impulse of any sane and rational person who is starting a new job is to fit in and align with the corporate culture. Likewise, there are many good reasons for the organization to have both a well-designed and well-executed new employee orientation *and* a structured probation period. These measures allow the new employee to have the greatest chance of long-term success and to quickly feel comfortable in the new role. To these ends, feedback is absolutely essential. The employee needs to receive reinforcement related to what he or she should be doing more or less of, and the organization needs to assess whether or not the employee is a long-term fit.

People are forever providing us with welcome and unwelcome information about our behavior, this practice is called feedback. Ideally, feedback is given to us to help us to improve our relationships, but as often as not, feedback is provided to make the speaker feel better without regard to whether or not the feedback is accurate, welcome, or in any way useful. I'm sure you can well imagine what outcomes you might experience if you give this type of scolding to an employee with a temper, difficulty with impulse control, and or propensity for violence. I am fond of saying being a—and I will clean this up for those of you with delicate sensibilities—jerk feels good for about 15 minutes, but the damage to the relationship can last decades (or a lot shorter if the offended party decides to kill you.) Seriously, as Maya Angelou said, "I've learned that people will forget what you said, people will forget what you did, but people will never forget how you made them feel," and the indelible wisdom of her words underscores the importance of properly administering feedback. Feedback needs to be more than information about your behavior. Hell, everything from bullying to scolding to being insulted can be information about your behavior, and (before you dismiss it too quickly) if you have ever taken a well executed right hook to the temple after behaving in a particular way (as I have,) you know that the person throwing the punch was made to feel humiliated, insulted, threatened, or any number of unpleasant emotions. And believe me when I say that while you may be left wondering precisely how you made the person feel, chances are you won't have the opportunity for many follow-up questions.

On a related note, bullying, which is directly related to the topic of this book, is about the abuse of power. My dear departed mother always used to tell me to stand up to bullies because bullies are insecure and will respect you if you stand up to them. For the record, bullies choose victims that they are absolutely, positively certain they can take in a fight—on the playground and in the boardroom. As for my mother's advice, it didn't work and I concluded a long time ago that my mom just liked to see me get a good asskicking every once in a while. The term bullying has been broadened to the point that if someone looks cross eyed at someone else, inevitably some dimwit will label the behavior as bullying. This broadening of the definition cheapens and weakens the seriousness of the problem of bullying. Not all inappropriate behavior is bullying and to a large extent, the decision as to whether or not someone is or has been bullied has to be made by the person who is the target of the aggressive behavior.

Bullying is the practice of attacking someone from a position of power, leaving the victim with little recourse other than to put up with the behavior. On the playground, the bigger, sadistic, and socially maladroit kids will invariably pick on the smaller, weaker, and more passive kids (ironically the victims are often socially maladjusted—a small kid with plenty of friends is not likely to be bullied.) Bullying is pack behavior, and while society may label it learned behavior the fact is people are predators and the instinct to prey on the weak is ingrained. With that having been said, society imposes consequences on bullies and when these consequences are sufficiently unpleasant the bully will generally abandon the behavior; this may be the one aspect of safety and violence where I believe behavior modification can make a difference. Let's not give bullies an excuse to bully. They don't need counseling to understand right and wrong; they need others to stop rewarding the bullying behavior. A bully that is socially ostracized will generally stop bullying, but a bully who tortures a weaker kid while the other kids laugh and cheer will be emboldened to repeat this behavior.

When bullying enters the workplace, things get more complicated. Remember true bullying isn't just being mean to someone, it's being mean to someone who can't realistically fight back. If a coworker continues aggressive behavior toward a victim, the victim can report it to the appropriate corporate authorities and if sufficient action is not taken the victim may—depending on the nature of the bullying—have legal remedies at his or her disposal.

A Tale of Two Bosses

I've had plenty of bosses in my storied career, some good, some bad. Of all the people for whom I have worked, however, two stand out as exemplary—one extremely good and the other extremely bad.

"Gary" was an executive who was one of my internal customers. Gary and I had a good rapport and Gary delighted in remarking on my wardrobe that was technically compliant with the dress code but was always eye-catching, from my black on black on black suit, shirt, and tie combo to my bright purple suit respite with a Dilbert tie. Gary always had something to say about the way I was dressed and I would always give him a slow look up and down before saying, "fashion tips mean so much coming from you," to which he would guffaw. There was nothing mean-spirited in our comments to each other. One day, after a corporate restructuring, (we used to call it rearranging the deck chairs on the Titanic) I ended up working for Gary. When I showed up one day wearing some bizarre outfit, Gary grinned and made some comment like he always did. Then he caught himself and he began tripping over himself apologizing. I told him it was okay, that we always joke around like that. He told me that, no, it was not okay because I was his boss and while he could say whatever he wanted, I had to hold my tongue or face potential disciplinary, financial, or even punitive consequences. He told me that a boss can never insult—even jokingly—because the boss has an unfair advantage and it is an abuse of power. That exchange with Gary stuck with me from that day forward and remains the best example of corporate bullying that I have ever heard (don't get me wrong, I have taught sexual harassment avoidance for many years, but there is a threshold between friendly banter and bullying and a bigger threshold between bullying and harrassment; all inappropriate banter is not bullying or harrassment, but all of it should be addressed.)

Years later I went to work for "Milt." Milt was a corporate bully and a jerk. He ignored the rules when they didn't suit him—from smoking in the office to sexual harassment—but would hammer anyone who dared to disobey corporate policy. He would go so far as to walk around the office on Friday afternoons to see who left early (at one point I asked him how much the company was paying him to walk around taking attendance and if he really thought this was the best use of his time. He just harrumphed and stomped away.) It's worth noting that the employees on which he was checking weren't HIS employees, so why did he do it? Because he could. I never saw Milt work a weekend, stay later than 5:00 p.m., or even show up for work on time.

Milt inherited me when my boss left the firm to care for his ailing wife. Milt made it a point to demonstrate his power over me to the point where it would not have surprised me if he had tried to dry hump my leg. Milt was forever alpha dogging me, daily telling me that I better sell something or I would be out of a job (very helpful coaching, prior to this I thought that the company could survive with absolutely no customers or money coming in.) All of Milt's efforts to cow me into submission were in vain. He was lazy, slovenly, abrasive and what I called an "on-the-job retiree." Before working for him, I genuinely liked Milt, but after working for him I could barely stand breathing the same air as him. The threat of firing was ever present. The final straw was when I told Milt that I would be late because I would be attending the funeral of a close family friend. He got irate and told me that he needed me in at 9:00 a.m. for a meeting and furthermore, if I was in at 9:01 I was fired. I told my departed friend's family that I could not be a pallbearer at the funeral and in fact, I wouldn't be able to attend at all.

I arrived at work at 8:30 a.m. without a clue as to what the meeting would be about. I went to Milt's office at about 8:55 and asked if he was ready for our 9:00 a.m. meeting. He looked at me quizzically and said, "what meeting?" At first I was confused, and said, ``the meeting that you said if I wasn't here for you would fire me!" Now I started to lose control—he had overplayed his hand and pushed his bullying too far. I continued, "the (expletive) meeting that I missed the (expletive) funeral of my friend for. The meeting that made me have to call my friend's family and tell them I couldn't be a pallbearer (string of colorful expletive adjectives followed by an even stronger expletive used as a noun)!!!" We were both screaming now. He started to answer me "Now, you listen here…" his voice trailed off. The look on my face was sheer, unadulterated murderous rage. In my mind, I quit at that moment. Milt's reign of terror and abuse was over. Now he was just a fat old man whose body and mind were desiccated by too much booze, too many filterless Camels, and an ego the size of Nebraska. There came a voice from the office doorway. The CEO asked in a raised voice what exactly was going on. I sputtered out what had happened as best as I could. The CEO looked at Milt and asked, in genuine wonder, what the hell Milt was thinking by deliberately making me choose between being at a pointless meeting and being a pallbearer at my friend's funeral. The CEO calmly asked me to go back to my office and calm down, and that he would be down to talk to me in a minute. As I left, Milt mumbled a weak "he never told me he was a pallbearer" and the CEO spit back "it doesn't matter! I can't believe you did this."

I went back to my office and began packing my things into a cardboard box that I had grabbed from the storeroom on my way. A short while later, the CEO entered my office. His voice and demeanor were calm. "I'm sorry for your loss, Phil. Was this a close friend?" I told him that she came to my house for dinner every holiday and while she wasn't a blood relative, yeah, I was close to her and Milt's behavior made the pain, loss, and helplessness one feels at the unexpected death of someone close to him or her was made exponentially worse. I told him that as far as I was concerned, Milt had done this to force me to quit and it had worked. The CEO sighed deeply and told me that effective that moment Milt was no longer my boss, and that he was seriously considering firing Milt. I said nothing. He asked me to please unpack my things, and said that if I agreed to stay I would be working for him from that point on. I stayed, but avoided Milt for the rest of my tenure at the company (which wasn't long.) The well had been poisoned, and even though I no longer worked for Milt I was determined to find another employer. When I was finally laid off a couple of months later, I started my own business and moved on physically and mentally. I was in the final stages of an exhaustive interview process with a large healthcare system and was out of work a total of less than three months (and my own business thrived.)

As an adult I have taken more than my fair share of bullying from pompous executives, customers, and even a bloated warthog of a coworker. With the exception of Milt, I never let it get to me. I would secretly think to myself, "you have an economic power over me now, but someday you will just be a jerk carrying a bag of groceries as I drive ever closer to you, mulling over the decision as to whether to hit the gas or the brake…(cut to a grocery bag spilling its contents on a parking lot, a single apple rolling as if fleeing in terror.) Of course I would never act on that urge, but it eases my anger, stress, and other negative emotions. But for some people this kind of thinking becomes an obsession, and then a plan, until, as the Boomtown Rats said, "the silicon chip inside her head gets switched to overload" and all hell breaks loose. So the point is to watch what you say when you are talking to people, and even when you need to correct someone there are effective and ineffective ways to provide information without sending an individual into a seething rage. In recognizing that there is a right and wrong way to provide feedback to a person about his or her behavior we should all make a concerted effort to provide clearer and more appropriate feedback. Remember, the point of giving feedback is to help a person perform better not to make ourselves feel better..

Types of Feedback

There are four basic types of feedback, and each has an appropriate use. These types are Silence, Criticism, Advice, and Reinforcement. It's strangely appropriate to use the mnemonic "SCAR" for feedback in the context of workplace violence because inappropriate feedback can indeed scar relationships, confidence, and work performance, or even our bodies.

Silence	Criticism
Appropriate Use: When emotions are running hot *Overuse Leads to:* Paranoia, damaged relationships	*Appropriate Use:* When there are no associated positive behaviors *Overuse Leads to:* Escape and avoidance, damaged relationships, outbursts of aggression or violence
Advice	**Reinforcement**
Appropriate Use: When the person does a good job most of the time but has a bad habit or two *Overuse Leads to:* SFT (let's not go there)	*Appropriate Use:* When behavior is outstanding and has no associated negative traits *Overuse Leads to:* Perception as condescending or insincere

Silence

Perhaps the most common form of feedback is silence. Silence could also be described as the absence of feedback when feedback is expected. This particular form of feedback is appropriate for the times in life where we want everything to stay the same. Has anyone ever asked you, "if you weren't happy, why didn't you say something?" If so, you were probably overusing feedback. Silence is often an excellent tool for remaining cool when your emotions are raging—when you are so emotionally overwrought that you are likely to say something that will only make the situation worse—but silence is a short-term fix.

We often use silence as a flight mechanism, we don't want to fight, so we mentally extricate ourselves from the situation by remaining silent. Rather than providing more direct feedback and potentially provoking further attack, we remain silent and let things simmer. Silence should be used sparingly; it hurts relationships as we ascribe sinister motives to the person from whom we receive no information. As our brains have only partial information with which to determine whether or not we are in danger, we react as if the silent ones are hostile to us. Many an employee inaccurately assumes that his or her boss doesn't like him or her simply because the employer has not provided enough reassurance to the contrary. Years ago, I had a job that required a heavy travel schedule, which in turn meant that I had very little contact with my boss. Soon I became convinced that my boss was out to get me, and that—despite constant praise from my customers, and positive performance reviews—I was in imminent danger of being fired. It is interesting to note that even though I was fully aware that my paranoia was a direct result of a lack of feedback from my boss, I was unable to shake my raging paranoia; my subconscious was far stronger than my intellect. (This is not something of which I am especially proud; let's just say I don't have it on my resume.) We may also become paranoid if the majority of the feedback is silence. If we feel out of the information loop, our brains, craving information with which to protect us, manufacture threats and plots against us. Again, the brain's "better safe than sorry" response prepares us for greater and greater threats that may not exist. I explore this in greater depth in my unpublished "Why Do We Tell Our Children Not To Take Candy From Strangers When Everyone Knows That Strangers Have The Best Candy?" Who knows, someday I may dust it off and con my publisher into putting it out there.

Criticism

The second type of feedback is criticism, and unfortunately it is probably the second most frequently used. Criticism is the practice of sharing negative information about us without any other information. Criticism is essentially an attack—someone tells us what we are doing is bad, wrong, or otherwise undesirable. Repeated criticism hurts relationships; a big surprise—we tend to dislike people who continually remind us of how stupid we are, how much we need to improve, or how foolish we've acted. I personally have taken no solace in someone kindly reminding me that my predicament is entirely of my own making. Thanks to all of you who have helped me on my journey to self awareness and improvement.

As we are in close proximity with people who criticize us, we are increasingly likely to employ a fight/flight response. If we spend enough time with the person and our fight response is engaged, it is highly likely that we will lash out at that person either overtly or covertly. An overt aggressive response can take the form of a verbal blow-up or in extreme cases, physical violence.

Take for example the case of the worker who is continually criticized by his boss. Day after day the boss nit-picks about the quality of the work. One day, the criticism becomes too much and the employee explodes in a flurry of obscenities he tells the boss with dubious anatomical accuracy specifically which orifices the boss can stick this month's status reports. I once observed to my boss that I only heard his nasally drone when I did something he didn't like. "Phiiiiiilllll…" it always began. I asked him if there wasn't anything, some small thing, that he thought I did satisfactorily (I dared not hope for something he liked.) He responded by whining that no one gave him any recognition and that I had members of the executive team single me out for my great work and that nobody ever told him that HE did a good job. I called him a fucking child and hung up on him. I left the expletive in because I think it is important for even the most easily offended among you to understand the intensity of how his feedback made me feel. Even cornered like a rat, this asshat could not think of a single positive thing to say about me or my work performance.

Aggression is far more likely to be covert. In the previous example, the employee became overtly hostile as his fight/flight lever got switched to fight. In a far more likely scenario, the employee becomes passive aggressive. Instead of obscenity and creative anatomical body packing, the injured employee takes the fight underground. Graffiti gets sprawled on bathroom walls; deadlines get "innocently" missed; key information is not conveyed and the employee engages in malicious obedience. Passive aggression doesn't relieve stress, however, and in many cases it leads to guilt as our stress level eventually subside. Sometimes criticism triggers the flight response; instead of fighting we flee. The flight response manifests itself in a phenomenon called escape and avoidance. In other words, we—often without realizing it—will quickly excuse ourselves from the company of [51]the person who over criticizes us (escape) or, when we are able, avoid contact with the criticizer altogether (avoidance.) My ex-wife and I used to like to play a little game we called "what's wrong with Phil?" The game began with her saying "you know what's wrong with you?" As much as I loved this game, (I actually lettered in it in high school) I found myself saying, "You know how I love this game, and how I thirst for information to help me on my road to development, however, I have pressing business elsewhere." It came as no surprise that I didn't want to listen to an attack on who I am as a person, but any response short of fleeing the scene is likely to provoke more, and escalate the criticism.

Sometimes the criticism is subtle, the person providing feedback isn't directly telling you that you're broken, they insinuate that you're broken: "You should buy a house; renting is for suckers." "You should sell real estate: there's good money in it." Did you

---

[51]*She died of a heroin overdose six years ago and is the subject of the book Loving An Addict: Collateral Damage Of the Opioid Epidemic, publication pending.*

ever notice how some people can make you feel like crap while sounding so very helpful? It's irritating and yet we feel guilty for being irritated since they were "only trying to help." The instances where people offer us help when we've never as much as hinted that we needed assistance are maddening. Why does it irritate us? They're just trying to help out, right? When someone tells us that we "should…" it is an act of aggression. For starters, they are attacking us under the guise of trying to help which, once again, triggers our flight or fight reflex. We go on alert, our brains flood our bodies with chemicals, and our bodies brace themselves for a fight. We respond with something like"you should shut the hell up and mind your own business" (fight) or "yeah, you're right" (flight.) When I train people in providing and receiving feedback I tell them that you should never let people "should" all over you. This dynamic changes when one person has a power—particularly an economic power over us.

However well intentioned, the people who provide us with unsolicited criticism cause us stress. The unspoken message in the "you should…" is that if you continue doing what you are doing, you are broken in some way. The more passive the aggression, the more alert our bodies become and the more stress-related problems we suffer as a result.

Criticism tends to eliminate related behaviors that we value. For example, let's say you are the first to arrive at the office every day and the task of making the coffee falls to you. You don't mind, you do it because you like drinking coffee, it's not hard to do, and you like helping out the group. Now, one day, I come up to you and say, "you know, I'm getting sick of having to put away the coffee filters, mopping up the little puddles you leave behind, and sweeping up coffee grounds. You'd think at your age you'd have learned to clean up after yourself." After my reproach of your coffee making, what are the chances that you will be making any coffee (safe for me to drink) anytime soon? Chances are great that you will either stop making coffee (flight), tell me that I can make the coffee from now on (fight), or continue making coffee but now deliberately leaving a bigger mess (passive aggression) In all these cases, the goal to get me to pick up after myself is left un-achieved, and in two thirds of the cases a highly desirable behavior falls along the wayside. Clearly, a feedback tool that does not trigger the fight/flight response is necessary.

Advice

Not all feedback is dysfunctional, in fact, good, constructive feedback is essential for lowering our stress. A far more effective feedback mechanism is advice. Where criticism is destructive and focuses on negative aspects, advice is the practice of providing a more balanced description of the behavior. When providing advice, we begin by discussing positive behaviors before discussing behaviors we would like to see changed. Our example of the coffee-making mess could have been handled using advice instead of criticism and would likely have a much more positive result.

Advice is especially important when you are dealing with a probationary employee. Remember the probationary period is stressful not just on the employee, but for you as well. The employee—assuming they are functioning at a professional level—is primarily concerned with learning the rules, both formal and informal, and needs feedback on both what he or she is doing well and what areas need work.

Going back to our coffee example, instead of complaining about the negative aspects of the coffee, I should have started by commenting on the things in your behavior that I valued before moving on to the behaviors I would like to see changed. "I want you to know that I love it that you make coffee everyday; I am NOT a morning person and I rely on that first cup of coffee. I also need your help. Often, the kitchen area is a mess, in a large part because of the coffee that you make. How can I help you to clean up after yourself?" I can already hear some of you laughing, "yeah right...they'll just say 'you clean it if it bothers you'"...Maybe, and if you lack that person's trust, probably. If you have an ulterior motive; definitely. But even here we can glean important insights into whether or not the probationary is a good fit culturally

If you are insincere in your praise, you create, what a friend of mine indelicately dubbed, the "shit-filled twinkie." The shit-filled twinkie is a comment that at first appears to be a compliment (a delicious-looking snack cake), but inside the compliment is an insult (need I further explain the analogy?) In the interest of decorum, let's refer to my friend's analogy as the SFT. SFTs are created because the speaker is just going through the motions of commenting on positive elements of the behavior. SFTs do more harm than good.

Far from being a SFT, the advice approach mends troubled relationships and helps to build trust. As you build trust, your stress level, and the stress level of the other person diminishes. Remember, though, building trust takes time. Initially, the person receiving the feedback is likely to resist this change and only through patient, consistent advice will the relationship ultimately be mended.

I realized that I was overusing advice when one day after praising one of my staff members on a truly remarkable job, she looked at me with a wary expression and said "but..." I felt awful. Here I was, trying to genuinely compliment her on a job well done, but I had overused advice so much that she was instinctively leery of my comments.

One employer had a format for providing advice that has stuck with me even though it's been a decade since I left the company in search of fame, fortune, loose women, and desolate living and finding only the last of these. The format works like this (after following all the rules of feedback): " (Name,) I really value (whatever you legitimately value in the person)[52] and[53] I think you can be even more effective if you (talk about the area you where would like to see the improvement.)" Always end the feedback session with, "what questions do you have for me?" and "thank you for allowing me to provide you with this feedback."

---

[52]*If you don't value anything about the subject of feedback then you probably don't know the person well enough to provide feedback. If this is the case, take time to talk to the person and ask them what (in a work context) are some of the things of which they are proud?*

[53]*ALWAYS use AND not BUT. The word "and" builds on the positive foundation you have built but the word "but" obviates the affirmation of what you value about the person and replaces it with essentially a criticism.*

Reinforcement

Reinforcement, in feedback terms, is the act of recognizing outstanding behavior. Reinforcement can often be simply recognizing stellar performance, and it can be used to increase desired behaviors. Basically, reinforcement is the proverbial "atta-boy".[54] Everyone—and I seldom speak in absolutes—likes confirmation that his or her behavior is appreciated, noticed, and valued. Also, people tend to like to know when they are on the right track. Reinforcement can be as simple as a sincere, meaningful compliment ("You did a really nice job on that project: you brought it in on time, on budget, and everyone loved the results,") or as sophisticated as an employee of the month award; it's a way of thanking people for doing things right, and letting them know you appreciate the progress they have made. While it is difficult to over use recognition, it is not impossible. I once had a boss who praised everything I did. It was off-putting because he would praise me for doing the most rudimentary task. I began to lose respect for him because I believed either he didn't understand my job well enough to know whether I did a good job or a bad job, or that he thought so little of my abilities that he expected me to sit around drooling on myself. While he didn't mean to be condescending, it felt like he was patronizing me. Also, when you reinforce a behavior you must take pains to be absolutely specific or you will risk inadvertently endorsing related undesirable behaviors.

The Importance of Being Specific

I understand that we covered this material when we discussed the rules of providing feedback, but this particular topic is important enough to revisit. Irrespective of the kind of feedback we provide, we need to be specific. It is unfair to expect people to respond favorably to vague feedback. "You know that thing that you're always doing, I hate that." What are we expected to do with this kind of feedback? Unless I know exactly what elements of my

---

[54]*Can I still say that without offending some overly sensitive addle headed ninny waiting to be offended so they can whine and screech?*

behavior you don't like, there is little I can do to change my behavior. Instead, we would be better served by saying, "I dislike it when you put your feet on the dinner table and I would like you to please stop that." Providing specific feedback means that you must speak from your knowledge-base about things that you have experienced and seen with your own eyes.

How do you respond to a policeman at the door (just for context I should tell you that my doormat says "Come back with a warrant") who tells you that some of the neighbors have complained about the stench coming from your garage? Clearly this is an attack and you are likely to respond either by fighting or fleeing. Many of us would ask, "which neighbors?" or "who's complaining?" It is difficult for us to assess the value and seriousness of the complaint unless we can "consider the source" or at very least put the complaint into some sort of context. If we don't know who the feedback is coming from, it's virtually the same as getting no feedback at all. We really should restrict our feedback to things we've observed, noticed, or experienced and leave hearsay out of our remarks.

I once worked for a small consulting company, and one day the owner of the company called me into his office. He told me that he had received complaints about how I interacted with others in the workplace, and he was concerned that it was creating a major disruption in the office. He directed me to meet one-on-one with each of my co-workers to discuss our relationships, what I could do to be more effective interpersonally, and how I could better relate to others in my office. I at first decided that I was not going to do this exercise; I had more than a pretty good idea of who was responsible, and I knew his backstabbing charges were unfounded. Upon reflection, I saw no alternative to doing what I was ordered to do; I couldn't afford to quit without another job and there wasn't sufficient time to stall until I found another job. So I made 18 appointments. I decided that I was going to use this experience as a learning tool and to go into it without preconceived notions, reasoning that if I really was an obnoxious boor incapable of even the most rudimentary social skills this would be a good way to gain feedback. I met with my co-workers and, after providing them background as to why I was meeting with them, asked all 18 the same three questions;

1. Would you please describe my interpersonal skills?

2. Are there specific instances where I mishandled an interaction between us which has diminished our relationship?

3. What advice would you give me so that I can be more effective in my business relationships?

For the record, I was not exactly a model co-worker in those days (pause for disbelieving gasps.) Opinionated, I tended to monopolize meetings, argue miniscule points, and demonstrate a host of dysfunctional behavior of which I am too ashamed to relate here. Suffice to say I was more than a little apprehensive about letting down my defenses and risk having my feelings hurt in the rush of negative feedback I was sure to encounter.

The results of my mini surveys astounded me. First, all but one of my co-workers were sickened that the owner of the company had forced me to do this exercise. Next, all but one of my co-workers offered sympathetic, constructive advice that I still follow to this day.

Also, all but one of my co-workers turned against the one co-worker, who, as I had always suspected, complained about me without any validity to his complaints. I submitted my report to the owner of the company and his conclusion was that the complaining coworker had interpersonal problems and needed to do the same exercise I had done. He refused, and left the company soon after. Had the company owner dealt with only those things he had observed (by his own admission he saw no problem in my behavior) I would have been spared the humiliation of conducting my one-on-one coaching. Additionally, while the results of this exercise benefited me personally, it destroyed the credibility of the owner, and created a serious lack of trust between the employees and the owner of the company. The company has since gone out of business, having lost its entire workforce except for the owner's two unqualified children. But enough about him, I am sure he is roasting in Hell by now.

Ironically, the most effective form of feedback I have ever encountered comes from a former employer in a faith-based not-for-profit healthcare system. Feedback is delivered using a very simple formula:

1. Describe something you value about the person.

2. Offer a way that the person might be even more effective.

If this sounds simple, it's because it is. But it is also one of the most initially difficult ways to give or receive feedback. It sounds something like this: "I value your creativity and the energy you put into your assignments and I think you may be more effective if you focused a bit more on the accuracy of your final deliverables." This takes all of the blame, excuses, supposition, and all the other baggage typically attached to feedback out of the conversation and allows for a sincere exchange of information. Words have power, and starting with something that you truly value about the person feels good. By saying "and I think you…" instead "but I think you…" you continue making the person feel good about themselves and your relationship with them. Saying "but" is akin to saying "forget all those nice things I just said and do this!" The former invites a productive conversation and the latter provokes an argument (even if the person doesn't vocalize his or her disagreement.)

1. **Ask permission to provide feedback.** Just because you have something that you want to say, doesn't mean I want—or have to—listen to it. You are entitled to your opinion, but I am entitled to decline listening to it. Opinions may not be welcome, opinions may not be accurate or based in reality. Opinions are not facts, and it may not be a good time for the person to hear your opinion. Your conclusions based on your opinions might be flat out wrong. And maybe you've spouted out so much dreck that is just hurtful language criticizing me that I no longer value your opinion. In short, not everyone cares about what you think.

Start your feedback by asking, "Can I give you some feedback?" You must be prepared to drop the conversation if the person says no, or looks very uncomfortable. Also, you should ask permission to provide positive feedback as well; trust me, people will be pleasantly surprised to hear nice things said after answering yes to that question.[55]

2. **Be timely.** I hate performance reviews despite the fact that for the most part I get extraordinary reviews. But nothing aggravates me more than hearing about how irritating you found it that I was late one day in March when it's now August. In fact, it makes you seem slow-witted and petty, which you probably are. You are trying to tell me that while for most of the year I have had great attendance, me coming in late that one day in March just ruined your whole spring. For greatest impact, provide the feedback as close as possible to the time the behavior occurred, but don't provide feedback when you are angry. If you come at someone hot, it undermines all the feedback because the recipient will likely believe that the problem is about something else, and by the way I'm late a lot and we both know it.

3. **Be specific.** Telling someone that they're "doing a good (or bad) job" doesn't really provide any information at all, and therefore it is a useless waste of time both yours and the person to whom you are giving feedback. You need to explain specifically what you like or want changed in a person's behavior (and sometimes both.)

4. **Concentrate on behaviors.** Telling someone that you don't like their attitude is really just a way of telling him or her "I don't like you." Attitudes are behavioral manifestations of emotions, and while we can't control our emotions, we can control our behavior. Is it really the attitude you don't like, or is it the behaviors (sarcasm,

---

[55] *Along those lines, I have never had a good conversation with a woman that began with "can we talk?" It's never about how my new shirt really accents my beautiful eyes.*

constant complaining, etc.)? I once worked alongside a man who hated his job, and yet he did exceptional work, never complained or bad-mouthed the company or coworkers. Did he have a bad attitude? Some would say yes, but I would say, who cares how he feels about his job as long as he does it and his feelings about his job do not affect the overall morale of the company.[56] Back then workplace violence wasn't taken all that seriously. In fact, given the response to my first book on the subject, *Lone Gunman: Rewriting the Handbook On Workplace Violence Prevention,* I don't think it is taken that seriously now.

5. **Use "I" Statements.** There are few things worse than having your boss say "People are telling me that you are..." The logical first response is to get defensive and ask "who has been saying these terrible things about me?" It's a fair question. Without knowing who provided the information, you don't have any context, and without context you can't tell your side of the story. Some people instinctively attribute their own observations into shadowy third-party sources; this is just cowardice. When providing feedback, it's important to speak in the first person, for example: "I overheard you talking to a customer on the phone and when you said 'well I don't care if you like it, that's our policy,' I found your behavior disrespectful and rude." By dealing with behaviors you have observed, you are more likely to have a deeper impact on the behavior and less excuse-making or diversions ("Who told you that!?")

Avoiding the use of "I" statements is just plain chickenshit and cowardice. It typically makes the person receiving your

---

[56] *(By the way, the only reason I knew he hated his job was because he told me in an eerily calm and friendly way that "one day I am going to come in here and kill all of you." Today that would cause me alarm and consternation, but I merely said to him, "Charley, I want you to remember two things: 1) I have always been nice to you and 2) I'm out on Tuesdays; I'll leave a list.*

passive bullshit angry, confused, and maybe even fearful. Just talk to the person grown-up to grown-up and don't beat around the bush. Choose the appropriate kind of feedback and frame the conversation accordingly.

6. **Don't Ascribe Motives To The Person's Behavior.** When someone begins a feedback session by saying something like "I know you hate meetings, and I know you find it challenging to..." the person giving the feedback is being presumptive and insulting. Nothing that that person says after a soliloquy about how I feel and why I behaved the way I did has any credibility, and they too come across as being chickenshit.

7. **Respect the person's privacy.** Getting feedback can elicit a range of emotions from embarrassment to fear to defensiveness to anger, so it's bad enough to get information without knowing precisely what will be said. But having a crowd of people looking on with mouths agape heightens our anxiety and makes us more defensive.Unless the behavior is so egregious that you must act immediately, don't provide feedback publicly. After asking if you can provide feedback, move to a quiet, private, and neutral area. This will allow you to respect the person's privacy but also, by moving to neutral turf, you level the playing field and allow the other person to provide you some feedback as well.

8. **Thank the person for allowing you to provide feedback.** Receiving feedback is never easy. Just the words "Can we talk?" or some similar lead-in to a feedback session can cause extreme stress. Allowing someone to provide you with feedback is an act of extreme generosity and you should acknowledge that generosity with an expression of immense gratitude.

Summary

A probationary period should be viewed as an "on-the-job interview." Because the probation period begins at the moment the employee is hired, it is difficult for the employee to claim that he or she was illegally discriminated against (they WERE hired after all) and it is equally difficult to claim wrongful discharge since they were hired on a probationary basis. Too often employers either skip the probationary period altogether or make it a meaningless exercise that does nothing but waste time. But, a well executed probation period can help decrease the risk of hiring someone who might later be a rampage killer.

Thought Starters

Why is feedback so important to probationary employees?

At what point should you terminate the probationary employee?

How often should the hiring manager conduct one-on-one coaching/feedback to the probationary employee?

Do you have an ethical responsibility to tell a probationary employee why their employment is being terminated?

Chapter 10: Spotting the Red Flags

Many rampage attacks are committed outside the killer's workplace, so why should we care about the behavior of employees? Well, for starters we have a lot more interaction with employees and coworkers than we do with our neighbors, and also because by identifying and conducting a meaningful intervention we may save the lives of strangers enjoying a concert, school children and teachers, and a host of other "soft targets" that the rampage killer might attack.

According to Andrew Arena, "No one can say with absolute certainty why someone goes from 'a quiet guy who was never any problem' to a rampage attacker." Even so, Arena is quick to list some of the most common red flags, " (probably the most typical are)

Certainly mental illness plays a role in many of these attacks, but then I don't know about you, but I haven't met many people who weren't mentally ill to one extent or another. And as Jonathan Gold points out, "Too many people jump to the 'mentally ill' conclusion when in fact we don't know if the attacker is sane or not; we can't know what is in the person's mind."

I had a law professor who summed up the insanity defense nicely: "In my opinion, anyone who kills someone is insane, but that in itself isn't enough to justify an acquittal on the grounds of temporary insanity. The fact is, there are many, MANY, mentally ill people who do not commit murder and are not a danger to themselves or others. The question is whether or not the killer knew what he or she was doing was wrong, and most insanity defenses fall apart because most people cannot demonstrate that they didn't understand that murder was wrong." Rampage attacks are the last-ditch attempt to create change; it is the act of someone who is typically very controlling and who feels that he is out of options. His life is most probably spiraling out of control.

Even though we can't accurately predict who will become a rampage killer, there are several characteristics that many rampage killers share:

- **A Specific Target**. As I have indicated, at least 51% of rampage killers have a specific target in mind, but that number is deceiving since we can't know the motivation of a mass-shooter who is killed in the event either by his own doing or by the actions of another.

- **Feelings Of Failure, Hopelessness, or Self Loathing.** Many teen rampage killers have kept notebooks about their fantasies about slaughtering people or posted cryptic messages on social media that hinted at their desire for notoriety. Some commit suicide, while a small percentage are seeking notoriety. They know they won't be drafted by a pro-sports franchise, or become a rock star, or an influencer, or a movie star, or anything that the average teenager fantasizes about. The self loathing leaves them with seemingly only one way to leave a lasting legacy: murder with as high a body count as possible. While this characteristic is especially prevalent in teenagers, adults are not immune to these feelings and these feelings can be a powerful motivation that can drive one to murder.

- **A Loner, Socially Stunted, or Marginalized.** Many rampaging killers are overcome by a feeling that they don't matter. Socially awkward, the rampaging killer has trouble with relationships and may well be bullied at school or work. Eventually, they may become comfortable being on the outside or (thanks to social media) find others who feel equally marginalized, disliked, or isolated. The pandemic taught many of us on how debilitating isolation can be, and we have seen an uptick in everything from drug and alcohol abuse to domestic violence to rampage attacks.

Andrew Arena adds two more qualities:

- **Disenfranchised.** Andrew Arena points to people who feel that they don't fit in with the larger population—when one doesn't feel accepted for who they are, eventually they find it difficult to empathize or care about how people react to their person's feelings or actions.

- **Perceived or real grievances.** "Obviously right-wing extremists are a threat for violence within the agitated, political landscape we face today. However, they seem to be more of a threat for a planned and focused event. Obviously, extremist groups do spawn 'lone wolf' attacks. This is true all along the political and religious spectrum."

To echo what Andrew Arena and Jonathan Gold have both said, we will likely never know what causes the quiet guy in Accounting to come unhinged and harm either himself or others. It's scary, but we just don't know for certain and it's likely that there are multiple causes and triggers.

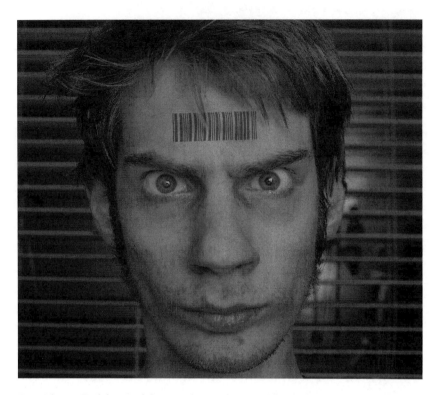

Jonathan Gold would seem to agree, "There is a lot of talk about these people being mentally ill, but we really can't make that conclusion since we don't know what is going on in the heads of the people committing these acts."

The rampage attacker is trying to exert the control he feels he's lost. My late father was very anti-litigious and he summed up lawsuits like this: "People sue when they don't feel like anyone is listening to them." I agree, but would add that people take extreme action when they feel like they have exhausted every other avenue.

Rampage violence is also typically carried out by individuals who are heavy alcohol or drug users (at least at the time of the attack— they may have been teetotalers before their lives took an ugly turn.) I think it's important to remind you that these red flags are correlations and not necessarily cause-and-effect. Plenty of people abuse alcohol and drugs and do not go on a killing spree. As stated, the perpetrators tend to be individuals who have been given every chance and typically are out of any sort of options. They carry a grudge for an injustice—real or imagined—and feel like they have no other alternative; they are cashing in their proverbial chips and going out in a blaze of glory[57] and gore.

Rampage violence is not typically motivated by hate, rather those who perpetuate these acts motivated by desperation and defeat or fueled by alcohol. Rampage killings in the workplace are the one last act used to demonstrate that the shooter still has some modicum of control over his life and the lives of his victims. Workplace violence seldom erupts without a string of warning signs—typically a small and seemingly petty or insignificant event like an insult or inappropriate behavior. You and your organization's ability to spot the warning signs–red flags–of a troubled employee (or a potential target) can mean the literal difference between life and a death. Treating any worker grievance—no matter how small or insignificant—seriously can actually be a matter of life and death.

Obviously, it's easier to deal with a tense situation using de-escalation techniques, but the secret to the success of these techniques is getting involved early; ignoring these warning signs can result in a situation that is much more difficult to deal with later.

What employees are most likely to become unhinged?

Of course, there are no perfect predictors of a rampage killer, but the key to preventing such attacks is to understand people's comfort zones. As I have stated at length, you shouldn't jump to any rash judgments about an individual just because of a couple of suspicious or odd behaviors. That having been said, some of the warning signs that an individual is becoming unstable (and these warning signs can apply to both perpetrators and targets) include:

---

[57] *Andrew Arena cautions against this conclusion, noting that while it certainly makes sense there is no empirical evidence that this is true. Thankfully, we do not have a large enough population to make statistically valid conclusions. Jonathan Gold puts it more succinctly, "we don't know what is going on in the heads of these people," says Gold*

Behavioral Changes

In most cases a rampage killer will exhibit easily observable behavioral changes long before actually acting, but to see these changes you need to know what "normal" behavior looks like. If you have been successful in weeding out undesirable and potentially dangerous candidates you may have seen some of these characteristics. But remember, as people settle into a new job, they tend to reveal things that may not truly be behavioral changes per se, rather they are personal attributes that the person was successful in hiding during the probationary period. For the purposes of this section I will not distinguish between the two. Some important behaviors and behavioral changes that you should look for include:

- **A marked change in personality**. One of the first and most notable changes that something is amiss in a person's life is a sudden and marked change in attitude. Someone suffering from outside stimuli that could trigger a violent episode often exhibit paradoxical changes in their behavior, particularly from friendly and sociable to sullen and antisocial, or from quiet and reserved to loud and bold. On the other hand, someone who is a potential target for violence may become withdrawn, quiet, and antisocial. This change in behavior can also indicate drug use, which in itself is also an indicator.

- **Becoming overly and inappropriately emotional**. What, you may ask, constitutes "inappropriate" behavior or becoming "overly emotional?" Crying over the loss of a parent is appropriately emotional, crying over the loss of a blue pen is not. To some extent, overly emotional is in the eye of the beholder. But when you view the behavior through the lens of workplace violence you need to concentrate on dramatic changes and subtle shifts in behavior. Often the feelings of hopelessness and loss of control that precede a rampage killing event result in emotional outbursts that are out of character, particularly angry outbursts, crying jags, or pouting. Just as when spotting liar's tells, the key is the sudden change, not merely the behavior alone.

- **Joking about or threatening violence.** Joking about violence means that, consciously or unconsciously, the person telling the joke is thinking about violence. Thinking about violence is not the same as planning violence, but it is another checkmark on our list of indicators. Threatening violence, even in a non-threatening tone, is far more serious and should be dealt with swiftly and decisively. These threats can be spoken or made through emails, in conversation, or subtle innuendo. I used to work with two men who both talked a lot about violence. One, a jovial coworker whose sense of humor held nothing sacred, openly speculated about his "kill route;" he wasn't serious, and we all knew it, but in retrospect, it probably was unwise for his coworkers and boss to ignore the gallows humor. The threat was not serious, credible, or alarming, and I think it illustrates nicely that someone who jokes about violence, more often than not, is not someone who will commit the acts about which he jokes. Then again, this scenario should be considered another red flag.

My brother recently died of a heat stroke that caused hyperthermia; it was sudden and tragic—the Hooterville (my hometown) police left his decaying body in his driveway, apparently poking it with a stick for six hours after the body was discovered in a misguided attempt to ascertain the cause of death. My surviving five siblings and I could agree only that he was dead. In short, it was a volatile and emotionally charged situation. In my text message to my boss, I explained what happened and I told him that I needed two days off...or more if I was incarcerated for killing one or more of my sisters. I tend to have a propensity toward gallows humor, but am not planning any immediate harm to any of my siblings. The point is that not all humor about violence results in violence, but it needs to be viewed in the context of the other red flags.

- **Persecution complexes and delusional thoughts**. The political climate in the U.S. and elsewhere, along with the proliferation of social media, has created the perfect breeding ground for delusional nut jobs. A worker who fails to acknowledge his or her drop in performance and blames others or claims that everyone is out to get them may be prone to violence—although generally speaking this is just a personality type and it's important to recognize that a *possibility* of violent behavior is not the same as a *propensity* for violent behavior, which is not the same as a *predictor* of violent behavior. These people will blame others for their mistakes and make repeated excuses. They may accuse their superiors of playing favorites or being "out to get" them. They will tend to look for reasons to take offense, and will often take things very personally. These people will deflect criticism by claiming that "everyone" is doing it and may actually believe that they are being singled out for punishment.

I once worked with a man who blew up and called a particularly loathsome customer a series of obscenities, many of which I am still looking up. The customer was predictably upset and called the president of the company. After conferring with the lawyers, they decided that this co-worker needed to be fired.[58] The confab took about three days, in which time this dysfunctional imbecile committed THREE additional fireable offenses including an incidence of sexual harassment! He was by all accounts a creepy little man who often expressed feelings of persecution and jealousy (and yet he felt others were jealous of his work and intellectual superiority—truthfully, I admit envying his command of obscenity; man, that guy could turn a colorful phrase!) Clearly this man should not have been hired, nor should he have been kept beyond his probationary period.

---

[58] *Yes, I know the absurdity of feeling as though you have to check with the lawyers before firing someone who did something like this.*

But as is so often the case with small companies, he was allowed to skulk around the office, creeping everyone out until he did the unforgivable: jeopardize a paying gig. What was most remarkable to me was when they fired him, he was astonished. He didn't see a single thing wrong with his behaviors. Fortunately for us, he left without incident.

- **Defiance of authority.** The typical rampage attacker holds grudges—especially against his or her supervisor—like a junkyard dog with a fresh bone. He or she will likely become openly defiant and voice his or her lack of respect for the company, the supervisor, and the executives. These types of people often will talk about the bad things that will happen to the person or people against whom they have grudges against by saying things like "don't worry, he'll get what's coming to him," or other ominous idioms. This defiance of authority may take the form of pushing the limits to test the extent to which the authority figure will allow them to behave dysfunctionally. What's worse is this defiance without consequence serves to embolden the behavior, inviting even greater demonstrations of defiance.

- **Recklessness.** The rampage killer has given up, and honestly doesn't consider or fear consequences. Long before this manifests in an actual violent episode, it will likely show itself in recklessness, from taking extreme risks in how they conduct business (like calling a customer obscene names) to theft or destruction of company property. In these extreme cases it's almost as if the individual is inviting a trigger, whether he knows it or not. This behavior, coupled with the other behavioral changes, is an observable prelude to a violent outburst.

- **Obsession with violent films or imagery.** Not everyone who is a fan of *A Clockwork Orange*[59] is a seething sociopath waiting to explode, but the person who is obsessed, and I chose that term carefully, with violence is

---

[59] *I have a framed reproduction of the movie poster on my bedroom wall. If it bothers my wife, she hasn't mentioned it.*

- more likely to perpetrate violence than someone who is not. Here again, the people obsessed with violence and gore who act on this are statistical outliers—if every immature man or adolescent boy who was extremely interested in violence went on murderous rampages there wouldn't be anyone left to kill. I am repeating this so often that it's getting on my OWN nerves, but one or two indicators does not a murderous maniac make.

- **Hostility toward women.** A disproportionate number of violent men have a deep-seated hostility toward women, particularly women in positions of authority. As I havee mentioned previously in this book, most rampage attacks have a specific target (or first target in mind). Of these intended targets most of these are women. Misogyny exists, and I don't get it. I have worked for many women over my long and storied career and actually preferred it (all it takes is one male jerk manager trying to alpha dog you and you learn to appreciate working for women.) I worked under one male executive that was so into demonstrating his power and authority that he would practically hump your leg when he came into the room, I don't mind telling you that not only did he create an uncomfortable work environment, but he made us all feel unsafe as he turned up the pressure on coworkers who we already considered dangerous.

When I tell some men that I worked for a woman, many of them are incredulous and openly say, "I could NEVER work for a woman!" I never understood this misogyny, and would usually deflect it by saying, "My mom was a woman, I have four older sisters, three daughters, and have been married twice, so I am used to being bossed around by

women. Frankly, getting paid for it is a nice change." Most women-hating men are savvy enough to keep their opinions to themselves, but they're still out there and they are potentially dangerous.

Physical Changes

I recognize that it is a fine line between physical and behavioral changes—one could argue that reporting for work unkempt and dirty is a behavior, while someone else could argue that these are physical changes. However you choose to characterize these changes, be alert for:

- **Poor hygiene, wearing dirty clothing.** It's one thing if someone has body odor from the day you hired them (and why for the love of all that's holy did you hire Stinky?) and quite another if the body odor develops suddenly and is in conjunction with other physical changes. Tread lightly here. You are within your rights to confront a worker about poor hygiene, but you cannot pry about physical conditions that might be causing said odors. Here again, there is a gulf of difference between Jimmy in the mailroom who likes to skip his morning shower and throw on yesterday's shirt so he can get an extra 10 minutes of sleep, and Joe the normally fastidiously dressed salesman who starts coming in one day looking like a mud wrestler and smelling like a honey dipper. In both cases, friendly, non-adversarial coaching is appropriate.

- **Bruising, cuts, or other indications of fighting.** While the first rule of *Fight Club* is you don't talk about *Fight Club*, you're not IN a fight club, you are in a position of authority and you have a responsibility to talk about what physical changes you have observed. Be sure that you don't interrogate the worker, but rather express–in compassionate terms–your concern for their well-being. Indications of fighting can be indicative of either an abusive or abused worker and in either case it should not be ignored.

- **Watery eyes and blotchy skin.** Watery eyes and blotchy skin can indicate a change in diet, physical illness or abuse, or drug/alcohol abuse. Together with these other indicators, they can add up to an unstable individual, or simply an insomniac. Either way, there is nothing wrong with a show of genuine concern, like asking, "Do you feel okay?"

- **Complaints about a vague feeling of illness or tiredness**. High levels of stress can manifest as vague aches and pains, lack of energy, or other ambiguous illnesses. Too often in our society, we dismiss an overly stressed worker as a hypochondriac or a crybaby. These symptoms are not imaginary, and lacking sympathy for the worker can be another paving stone in the road to an explosion. Also, a victim of domestic violence may exhibit these same symptoms. Intervening early can save lives.

Personality Styles and Their Roles In A Rampage Attack

Many of us are familiar with personality style inventories from DiSC to Myers Briggs, but my favorite work on the subject is *Personality Styles At Work: Making Bad Relationships Good and Good Relationships Better* by Robert Bolton and Dorothy Grover Bolton. What makes the Boltons' work interesting is their description of how an individual's personality styles change when the person is under stress and of course the very useful concept of flexing[60] (moving temporarily out of your comfort zone to meet another person in a neutral and less irritating zone). These personality inventories (or tests) are useful tools for helping people to recognize: a) people don't always see the world the way we do, b) our personality style is likely very different from the people we interact with daily, and c) our reactions to a situation or to another person's behaviors are not universal.

It's important at this point to address the major criticism of personality styles—that these types of tests (or inventories) are just a way to stereotype people. This criticism is not unfounded. I used to work for a person who was the human equivalent of a fetid, stinking bag of rancid bacon grease and eggshells. He was a retired U.S. army colonel who was the living embodiment of a person who simply couldn't adapt from the military into civilian life. Bereft of any real leadership or people skills, he would post his Myers Briggs profile on a cardboard nameplate he made. He would look at me and say, "We're never going to agree on this because I

---

[60] *One should not mistake flexing used in this concept (which is short for flexible) flexing a muscle (which means acting in a way that is aggressive, threatening, or intimidating.*

am an ISJ and you are an ENTP." This is asinine. He might as well have said we could never agree on something "because I am a Virgo and you are a Capricorn."

Each of us has a style of work and behavior in which we feel most comfortable. We also interact with people who have other styles of work, and our styles, while comfortable to us, are irritating to them. If we are going to be functional members of any community or organization, we have to find common ground with the people whose preferred style of work or communication differs from our own.

In the interest of brevity I will only deal with the four most common styles using the Boltons' terminology (the complexity of some of these personality style assessments is astounding.) The Boltons identify four basic styles—or as I like to say comfort zones—the circumstances and surroundings in which we are most relaxed and comfortable. These are: Amiables, Expressives, Drivers, and Analyticals. I am providing a 3,000 foot view of these so if you want more information, buy their two books.

Analyticals

Analytical people tend to be more comfortable being less assertive and less responsive than people who are comfortable in other environments. These people like rules, order, and logic and may become stressed in environments that are chaotic with lax enforcement of the rules. They are more adept at controlling their emotions and people who don't understand personality styles may describe this group—and even some people who are analyticals—as anal retentive. They like the order and predictability that rules and procedures seem to provide. Analyticals, along with Amiables, tend to avoid conflict and may be seen as inflexible bureaucrats. The stereotype for people in this comfort zone is the Accountant.

Amiable

People who are most comfortable pleasing people are referred to as Amiables. Like the Analytics, Amiables tend toward introversion and are less assertive than those in the other comfort zones, but unlike the Analytics, Amiables tend to be highly empathetic. People who are most comfortable in the Amiable classification are peacekeepers, and tend to be less assertive than others, but are team players. The Amiable is very open to the ideas of others and is generous with their time. The Amiable is sociable, but tends to forge deep relationships with a relatively few people. Amiables thrive in a highly structured environment and respect rules as a way of making sure that everyone is treated fairly (which they tend to define as everyone being treated the same, irrespective of the situation or circumstances) and their genuine concern for other people's feelings may be interpreted as weak, but that is a mistake. There is a danger that the Amiables' desire to avoid conflict will cause their ideas to either be ignored or not heard at all. The stereotype for Amiables is the Social Worker.

Expressive

Like those most relaxed in the Amiable comfort zone, Expressives love people and tend to be more open about their emotions than Analytics or Drivers. Expressives tend to be funny, talkative, and extremely social. Many people in the Expressive comfort zone need to talk to process information, and this can be perceived as flighty or unfocused by others. But telling an expressive to shut up (with your words or your actions) causes the Expressive to become very angry (in effect, the Expressive interprets that as being told to not think.) Expressives tend to use persuasion to get others to agree with them and don't care about the rules. The stereotype for the Expressives is the Salesperson.

Driver

The Driver comfort zone is characterized by people who are logical thinkers who make quick decisions. They are highly assertive but are emotionally restrained. Drivers can be seen as bullies by Amiables because Drivers tend to believe that the rules don't apply to them. The stereotype for this comfort zone is the Chairman. Drivers tend to be most comfortable being in charge and make decisions quickly. They are decisive and confident.

While each personality style has its strengths and weaknesses, most people tend to be a combination of two styles with one style being the primary comfort zone and the other being a secondary. There isn't a single personality style that is more prone to go on a rampage attack, so why talk about them here? Each of these styles tend to act very differently when under stress, and even MORE differently when under extreme stress. So by recognizing a person's comfort zone and traits when they are not under stress, noticing a change in behavior can help you to intercede and perhaps avert a tragedy.

Personality Styles Under Stress

Unlike many other authors on books related to personality styles, one of the things that I really find fascinating (and useful) about the Boltons' work is how personality styles manifest when people are under stress, and again when they are extremely stressed. While it is true that no one personality is more–or less–prone to committing a rampage attack, it is also true that a person that has been stressed to the breaking point is far more likely to go on a rampage than someone who is not at that point. Everyone occasionally suffers from excessive stress and in each personality style, this stress manifests differently.

Perhaps what is most important is to encourage everyone in the organization to act if they see something suspicious; to say something to a person in authority, and in extreme cases do something like getting to safety or monitoring the situation until help arrives. Everyone should be trained to recognize these red flags, reminded to treat the individual with compassion, and encouraged to report their observations to someone trained to handle these situations.

Analyticals Under Stress

People who prefer to function in the analytic comfort zones tend to retreat to an extreme version of their non-stressed self—they avoid contact with others, become quiet and withdrawn, and show far less emotion than they ordinarily would. Some may cut off social ties and spend long periods of time alone.

When the stress continues unabated, Analyticals retreat into what the Boltons refer to as their "secondary back up style." This secondary back up style is characterized by domineering, autocratic behavior. It doesn't take a lot of imagination to envision a scenario where this type of behavior could, at one extreme, aggravate a potential rampage killer and at the other end of the spectrum, trigger the rampage.

Amiables Under Stress

Amiables—ordinarily natural people pleasers—become even more so while under stress. This extreme niceness may confuse people of other personality styles into thinking that there is nothing wrong and that the Amiable is not only stress-free, but actually happy with the situation. But as the stress continues and the Amiable is forced into a secondary backup mode, the Amiable lashes out in a shocking wave of vitriol and potentially violence—if not physical, certainly verbal. This may explain (in part) why so many rampage killers are so often described as quiet, nice, people who generally kept to themselves.

Expressives Under Stress

Expressives under stress attack, sometimes viciously and mercilessly; they tend to say things that they regret after an explosion of anger and verbal assaults. But, when stressed even more, the expressive personality style will become disengaged and acquiescing. People of this style, when stressed to the max, tend to adopt a "Screw it. Do what you want" attitude. This can be startling or even dangerous for people of other comfort zones because as the stress eases, the Expressive returns to the rage that characterized the previous stress level.

Drivers Under Stress

People whose primary comfort zone is Driver become autocratic and outwardly obsessed with the letter of the law when under stress, even becoming tyrannical. For these people, stress levels would ease if others would simply follow the rules, without exception, complaint, or deviation. Drivers under stress may see noncompliance as a challenge to their positions or power which in turn is likely to cause them even greater stress. This increase in stress may cause the driver to become even more obsessed with rules and make decisions that they otherwise would see as unfair.

It is important to remember that it is rare for any of us to be at are best and for us to behave in ways of which we are proud when under stress. For my part, I have been training people how to improve their relationships with others using personality styles and flexing for over two decades and—even though I know the dynamics involved—still will behave dysfunctionally when I am under stress despite my best efforts to avoid doing so.

I really can't say enough good things about Robert and Dorothy Grover Bolton's work, I strongly recommend that you (if you haven't already done so) pick up a copy of their books. In addition to helping you understand what I dubbed your comfort zones, it will also help you to define the comfort zones of those around you and to flex—that is, temporarily move a bit out of your comfort zone to meet another on neutral ground—to those who have different comfort zones.

Personality Styles And Their Relationship With Violence

What I love most about the Bolton's view of personality styles is that they strongly stress that these personality styles are merely how a person prefers to operate and how a person sees their ideal surroundings and circumstances. They (and others) are careful to emphasize that personality styles aren't like astrological signs. You aren't destined to always behave in the ways described in works about personality styles.

So which personality style is most likely to become a rampage killer? Which is least likely to explode and kill people? None of them…and all of them. No single personality style is a predictor of a propensity for violence. So why did I mention it? Don't I have enough in this blasted book without including non-related material? Do I get paid by the word? The reason it is important to know your own and other's personality style is that by knowing people's response to stress, and even more importantly to extreme stress, you can intervene earlier and help the person lower and/or manage their stress and in some extreme cases maybe even avert a killing spree.

Summary

Most workplace violence is preceded by both physical and behavioral changes on the part of the rampage killer. Too often these "red flags" are ignored because a lot of people don't feel comfortable talking to someone who is obviously going through a rough patch. Countless news coverage of rampage killings feature witnesses and survivors describing the killer either as "the last person you would expect to do something like this" or "he was always creepy...there was just something about him that just felt off." In both cases the people describing the rampage killer saw the signs and ignored them. No one can afford to ignore these red flags.

Personality styles are good predictors of a person's stress level and when they might become dangerous because of extreme stress. Understanding a person's "comfort zone" can be key to intervening early and avoiding a disaster.

Thought Starters

Not all people who exhibit red flags will go on a killing rampage. In fact, only a relatively few do. What are some other ways a person who exhibits these changes might behave?

Eventually, you may have to terminate a troubled worker's employment. What steps should you take before doing so?

How would you determine "normal" behaviors of an employee or coworker?

What can companies do to meaningfully intervene to avert an employee who is at risk of perpetrating a rampage attack? What makes an intervention "meaningful?"

Rampage attacks are often an outgrowth of domestic violence, or domestic violence becomes a component of the person's

downward spiral. To what extent do you believe an employer has to intervene in cases where domestic violence is suspected?

What are some ways you can determine a person's personality style? How important is this, and why?

Chapter 11: Work Environments That Can Trigger An Event

I have worked in my fair share of toxic work environments, and in at least four of them there has been a workplace homicide (two of the shootings occurred after I no longer worked at the companies, and in two cases the murder victims were ambushed off site.) In all the incidents that happened in workplaces I worked or had worked, the motive was all the same: a lover's triangle.

Extramarital affairs tend to be a strong and extremely common cause of workplace violence and even seemingly random rampage attacks. My own marriage broke up as a result of my ex-wife cheating on me with at least one of her coworkers. I can tell you first-hand that such an experience isn't any kind of fun, in fact it's as close to hell as I ever want to come. But that was over 30 years ago, and in deference to my daughters' privacy I will spare you the gory details of the rest of my ex-wife's life (that ended abruptly six years ago.) Karma always seems to exact a horrible price.

In this chapter I will deal with four types of toxic cultures: the dating game culture, the tyrant culture, the frat house culture, and the pressure cooker.

The Dating Game Culture

There is a strange dichotomy in the law regarding dating in the workplace. On one hand, courts have upheld employees' right to date one another (although to call these rulings murky is to do mud an injustice) and on the other hand, workplace romances gone wrong are some of the most common causes of workplace violence, especially if the woman (almost exclusively) is married or divorcing her spouse. The wronged husband or cheated-on boyfriend, whose life is spiraling out of control, gets a couple of drinks in him, loads up the gun, and heads to the one place his intended targets will surely be: at work.

The shooter tends to kill the woman, her current paramour, and the boss for good measure (typically, the shooter has a less than amicable opinion of bosses in general and what the hell, he bought six bullets...) Seriously though, why a rampage killer—remember in most cases the killer has a specific target in mind—tends to bring multiple weapons and way more ammunition than he needs remains an enigma.

In many of these relationship driven attacks, good samaritansget caught in the crossfire and the gunmen, in a final act of complete control, commits suicide. So, what can you do to prevent this? Focus exclusively on work performance. I have yet to see a workplace romance that wasn't widely known and disruptive. I worked at one company where one department had more sexual activity going on than the court of Caligula. Eunuch managers whine that "there's nothing I can do...we don't have a policy," to which I would always reply (and forgive my crude language, but if you are that sensitive seriously why are you reading this?) "We don't have a policy against me shitting in your waste basket, but if I kept doing it you would find a way to get me to stop." We'll cover more about policies that you can enact in a later chapter, but in general, you can shut down the dating game culture by focusing on tangentially related behaviors where the dating of coworkers becomes problematic not because they're dating, but because they are acting like imbeciles. I know of one case where a married executive was having an affair with his married secretary.

The murky waters around the legality of disciplining employees for dating caused the legal council to get creative. Eventually, both were fired for cause...for misuse of office equipment. I wish this anecdote was a lot more juicy than it is, but the fact is the two were engaging in obscene phone calls with one another using their company phones. The policy on phone usage was clear: your business telephone was exclusively for business purposes and any other use was considered a misuse of office equipment, which was a fireable offense. This was an extreme case and it probably had more to do with avoiding a large severance package (fired for cause meant the offending party forfeited the right to a severance package) than the dating, but dating in the workplace opens up a Pandora's Box of workplace risks, from sexual harassment to workplace violence, so it cannot be ignored and must be managed carefully.

I used to supervise a young, friendly, upbeat woman just starting her career. A day didn't go by where men contrived reasons to talk to her. Although she did nothing to knowingly encourage them (she was fairly naive) the whole scene reminded me of when my childhood dog went into heat and dogs (who, let's face it,she was so far out of their leagues that they didn't have a chance) came from all over the county to pitch their woo. I sat her (my employee, not my dog) down and talked to her. I explained that she had done nothing wrong, BUT her gentlemen callers were preventing HER from getting her work done and preventing THEM from getting their work done. I further explained that if she wished to see any of them socially, she should accept invitations for lunch, but she needed to let them know that apart from her lunch break she was not interested in having them visit her in her work area. This cleared the issue up nicely. I dealt with work and performance issues, and only those. If she didn't like it, she never said anything about it, and frankly, it didn't matter, she was not paid to flirt, and her erstwhile gentlemen callers weren't being paid to walk around like Lotharios walking around the hotel bar at happy hour. The bottom line is only in very select occupations is anyone paid to flirt.

The Tyrant Culture

Unfortunately, I have worked in more than one Tyrant Culture. Most of you can probably relate to the bully-boy boss who gets his or her jollies from sending people fleeing his or her office in terror.

Bullies, contrary to popular belief, aren't stupid.[61] It's bad enough when it's on the school playground.[62] But as bad as that was, iit is far worse when the bully in your life has an economic power over you.

For some of us it's easy; you just quit. Or, you do like I do. Years ago, I had a customer who was off his nut and in full-on bullying mode. He was frothing at the mouth and screaming at me for doing exactly what he had asked me to do (and doing it well, quite frankly.) I simply sat back and gave him a sublime Mona Lisa smile. After the meeting, my boss was outraged. He swore that he was going to march into this man's boss's office and demand some vague form of justice. Then he got a good look at me, smiling like Johnny Depp portraying Ed Wood. The grin of a simpleton with knowledge no one else has. "Why aren't you angry?" my boss demanded. I said, "Easy. I realize that he has all the power now, but someday, maybe quite soon, he'll just be a guy. He won't have an economic power over me. We'll just be two guys. Maybe I'll be driving through a shopping center parking lot and maybe he'll be pushing a cart down the aisle. He'll look up and he'll see me, and the diabolical look on my face, as I bear down on him. And in that instant, he'll know true fear."

Most of us have these fantasies and that is why I will never win the lottery—too many revenge fantasies. But that's all they are, fantasies. I will never act on them and hopefully, none of you reading this will either. Sometimes it's healthy to blow off some imaginary steam, whether it's pretending the box you are punching to break it down for recycling is your boss's head or playing a violent video game. You and I know the difference between fake violence and actual violence, but for the rampage killers these aren't fantasies. They are, if not plans, then thumbnail sketches of what they will do to this tyrant once the bully pushes things too far.

---

[61] *Well at least not stupid enough to pick on someone who has a sporting chance of winning a fight or*

[62] *even inflicting serious harm.*

My grade school playground was a blacktop parking lot with no playground equipment surrounded by a 10-foot chain link fence complete with barbed wire atop. It was as close to the prison yard as I care to get (seriously, all that was missing was ethnic gangs and an area for weight lifting and they could move the convicts in tomorrow.)

Obviously, they know they won't be able to drag the red-faced, fat-assed CEO dictator into the pit they dug in the basement and force them "to rub the lotion on its skin or it gets the hose again." But he knows that he has a gun and a singularity of purpose for that one last great act of defiance.

Another Tyrant boss who I still refer to as The Devil was an ex career military officer who demanded that his (usually imbecilic) commands were carried out without deviation or argument. So I would follow his orders knowing full well that he either lacked a key bit of information or that his idea would backfire with disastrous results. One day he called me into his office and sat me down. He accused me of "malicious obedience." I had never heard the term, so he explained that I was guilty of subverting the spirit of his "instructions" by carrying them out as directed. I responded by saying that I routinely did as he described and would continue to do so as long as he refused to listen to my protestations. I explained that when I resisted his commands, it wasn't because I was lazy, defiant, or (heaven help me) challenging his authority, but trying to warn him of the logical consequences of his own stupidity (I cleaned that last part up.)

The abuse didn't come from The Devil alone; through his example, he made violence against coworkers acceptable, even encouraged. I remember an instance when during a meeting, I kept asking a coworker whose first language was not English to repeat himself. He was far behind on his project and the continued berating by the Devil made his already fairly thick accent even more difficult to understand. For the record I was not mocking, bullying, or berating him in any way, I simply could NOT understand what he was saying (the fact that he was at the far end of the room from me didn't help matters) and needed the information to do my job.

The meeting was tense, and he was noticeably frustrated. When the meeting broke up he casually said, "You know, someday someone's going to beat the crap out of you for your smart mouth." In an offhand response, I said, "Well, not today." This enraged him, and as soon as I turned my back, he jumped on me and punched me,screaming, "Don't be so sure!" Fortunately for me, the bulk of the meeting attendees, mostly men, subdued him by throwing him to the ground and holding him until he got his temper under control.

Keep in mind, this gentleman criminally battered me without any deliberate or serious provocation in front of The Devil, who did and said nothing. There were no work consequences—soon after he apologized, and I told him that I was not trying to embarrass him but couldn't understand him. He asked if I was going to file charges, and I said that I wouldn't THIS time, but that he should not mistake mercy for weakness.

A few weeks later, he blew up at another coworker who fled the office before there was any violence. The violent offender, sure that the other employee would insist he be dismissed, went in and told The Devil off and quit. I steered clear of the office for a week or so to be sure he wasn't coming back—security was lax. Discretion being the better part of valor,I decided that it would be wise to avoid the office until things cooled down.

Shortly before I left the company, an apparently random shooter fired two shots into The Devil's moving vehicle. No one was harmed, but it was enough to shock him into somewhat less tyrannical behavior (for the record I have an alibi.) I was never completely convinced that he was shot at and even if someone did shoot at his car, I didn't believe someone would have the wherewithal to identify him as the intended target, but two windows were shattered as he drove down the freeway and what's more important is that HE believed an attempt had been made.

As the small company he founded disintegrated, he was legitimately surprised that the people he had routinely mistreated left the company either taking key clients with them or joining the client organizations and devoting their lives to ensuring that the client never did business with him again. Unfortunately, too often the proverbial straw that breaks the camel's back doesn't come from the Tyrant, rather it is the bearer of bad news. The pallid supervisor who delivers the bad news that vacations have all been put on hold, or that raises and bonuses will be delayed by six months, or whatever triggers the gunman into doing something egregious enough to get fired. I know one executive who openly bragged that he would fire the people who performed in the lowest ten percentile of the company he ran irrespective of whether they met their goals or not. He was (and if the miserable jerk is still alive probably still is) a bully and proud of it. He drove good people from the companies he ran, but for whatever reason (one can only assume blackmail) he has kept his job.

The executive bully makes the decisions that are carried out by others, who are then put at risk because typically the bully is so insulated from the unstable person that he or she doesn't recognize the danger in which he or she places the rank and file, and if he or she did, the executive bully isn't likely to care. The person who must deliver the bad news is put in the untenable position of being forced to deliver bad news to people he or she knows will react badly. The supervisor is typically equally affected by the decision and doesn't like the news any more than the recipients, but it's part of the job and not doing it will bring the wrath of the Tyrant. Sadly, the bearer of bad news, in the Tyrant Culture, is typically one of the first to die.

The Frat House Culture

The Frat House Culture is characterized by man-children behaving badly. The denigration of women is seldom subtle, and even Human Resources takes a "laissez faire" attitude of "boys will be boys." In this environment, professionalism is practically nonexistent and just like a poorly disciplined fraternity, hazing, bullying, and establishing a pecking order are common (if not pervasive.)

In the Frat House Culture, bad actors are often protected by executives and the result can create a powder keg environment. When a woman is having marital problems, one or more of the "frat brothers" will swoop in with a sympathetic shoulder on which to cry. The situation can be made even worse when an emotionally troubled woman chooses to get romantically involved with someone in a position of power in an effort to advance her career (personally I never had such an issue since the number of women willing to sleep their way to the bottom part of the middle is very low.)

Their tends to be a lot of flirting, open extramarital affairs, and sexual harassment in organizations with a Frat House culture. Not only are these conditions ripe for creating the conditions of a rampage attack, they are also likely to be considered by the courts as a hostile workplace (a type of sexual harassment for which the organization is always accountable and responsible.)

Central to the Frat House Culture is the idea of belonging to an exclusive group that is a subset of the larger population. Those in the elite subset practice organizational omerta—even those who are innocent of any wrongdoing are bound by this code of silence and the knowledge that no one that matters will say or do anything enables the bad actors. Too often people (both men and women) will tolerate or even encourage inappropriate behavior to curry favor with the inner circle.

Meanwhile the estranged partner or husband feels that he can't compete with a man outside his societal station and reasons that while he may not have money, fancy clothes, or a country club membership he does have a Glock, a fifth of Old Granddad, and the guts to show those people his power.

The Pressure Cooker

When most of us think of the Pressure Cooker work environment, we think of the high-stakes and fast pace of Wall Street or something similar, but in many cultures, there is a pervasive feeling that you're only as good as your last sale or project and that your job hangs by a thread. The Pressure Cooker culture can be created when workers come to believe that if they aren't pushing themselves to the breaking point, their bosses will believe that they need more work. No one can work at 100% capacity at all times, and in fact, no one can work at 100% capacity for very long at all.

Working at or near your capacity leads to stress, fatigue, and physical, mental, and emotional exhaustion. The adage "blowing off some steam" comes from the pressure valve on steam engines that were designed to release the steam, to prevent the built up pressure from causing the steam engine to explode. There is a similar valve on the top of a pressure cooker. A heavy, metal engine or pot made of thick metal literally exploding because of too much pent up steam is an apt analogy to this kind of workplace.

The bosses in these environments cultivate a chronic sense of unease and high stress—the harder they push people, the more money they themselves make. As I indicated, I worked at a place where one top executive openly bragged about firing the lowest

10% of performers. This human leaking colonoscopy bag of excrement thought that this made him look like a tough leader, when in fact, it just sapped the motivation of the workforce and drove fear to every area of the company. For the Pressure Cooker to take hold, the managers must simultaneously convince the workers that they will never have things as good anywhere else as they do at their current position. I have been made to feel this way by an employer or two, but when I left these environments I ultimately found a better job that paid more and had better benefits and working conditions. But not everyone feels comfortable making that kind of a move. In fact, the idea that "if you leave here, you will regret it" only reinforces unstable people believing that they are out of options. Eventually, a worker snaps and explodes. Most don't go on a killing spree, but companies that perpetuate this Pressure Cooker environment are basically daring a worker to go on a rampage.

Other Cultural Considerations

I get a bit tired of people blaming everything on the corporate culture because I think it tends to obviate people from their personal accountability and responsibility. I mean, if it is all about culture then what can I do, right? The reality is that everyone in the organization contributes to the corporate culture, and while changing an organization is like trying to change the course of an ocean liner, each of us can play a meaningful role in influencing not just the culture of the workplace but also of our communities and virtually all the people we interact with on a day-to-day basis. You send out stimuli, and people—usually without making a conscious decision to do so—react in some way. If you control the stimuli you send out ,you influence the response you get. Sending out a positive and compassionate message may just alter the trajectory of the life of a potential rampage killer; you never know.

The Shadow Of the Leader

Years ago I wrote an article in a magazine titled, "You Get What You Put Up With." I think the title alone sums up corporate culture and everything from customer service to interpersonal relationships. When a person acts in a dysfunctional way and you say nothing, you are not only condoning that behavior, but you are also encouraging it.

I have had C+ leaders complain to me that two or more of their top people are constantly (and publicly) behaving badly—shouting matches, outbursts in meetings, etc. I tell the executive that the choice is easy: either fire both of them or accept the fact that they will let two dysfunctional idiots lead the organization.

Not all bullies are at the top of the organization; anyone at any level can be a bully. Bullying in the workplace, particularly by a supervisor, can be subtle or overt, but if it is tolerated then the bully is emboldened to escalate his or her behavior. People take their cues from the leaders of the organization (nobody ever wrote a bestseller called "Dress for Complete and Utter Failure.") The key to achieving success in an organization is to curry favor by imitating the leader —this phenomenon is often referred to as "The

Shadow of the Leader" and it can be powerful and pervasive in a corporate culture.

As someone once said to me, "What the admiral finds interesting, the rest of us find fascinating." There's good news in this because while a bullying boss can create a climate of fear, a kind and nurturing boss can not only tear down a culture of tyranny but can build a culture that demands respect for subordinates and peers.

The shadow of the leader can also lead to peer-to-peer bullying even if the leader him/herself is not a bully. All that needs to happen for peer-to-peer bullying to happen is for it to be condoned or ignored by the management team. Too often first line supervisors are promoted from within and give little to no management training. First-line supervisors are typically promoted to a supervisory role because they are punctual, do their jobs, mind their own business, and keep their mouths shut. While these are valuable skills they are not necessarily the skills one wants in a supervisor. For example, I once worked in a factory where horseplay was prevalent. I learned very quickly to speak up and to tell the handful of offenders to knock it off or face the consequences, but some of the less assertive workers endured practical jokes and harassment in silence. This horseplay and practical jokes were happening right under the supervisor's nose and since it went uncorrected others started to join in the harassment until one of the victims filed a complaint and it could no longer be ignored,

Crafting A Calming Culture

For a relatively brief portion of my career I worked in a not-for-profit, faith-based health care system. The origins of this organization is the stuff of fairy tales except for the utmost important fact that this origin just so happens to be true. Several decades ago, two religious orders that ran hospitals realized that the youngest member of either order was 78 years old. The orders needed to act fast—not just because together they ran over 100 hospitals, but because the culture that they had crafted for over 600 years was on the verge of extinction. To survive they had to do the unthinkable: turn the culture over to laypeople.

The orders merged and created a steering committee that created a faith-based organization with a clear mission ("We...serve together in the spirit of the Gospel as a compassionate and transforming healing presence within our communities.") Core Values ("**Reverence:** We honor the sacredness and dignity of every person. **Commitment to Those Who are Poor**: We stand with and serve those who are poor, especially those most vulnerable. **Safety:** We embrace a culture that prevents harm and nurtures a healing, safe environment for all. **Justice:** We foster right relationships to promote the common good, including sustainability of Earth. **Stewardship**: We honor our heritage and hold ourselves accountable for the human, financial and natural resources entrusted to our care. **Integrity:** We are faithful to who we say we are."[63]) and "Guiding Behaviors:

- We support each other in serving our patients and communities.

- We communicate openly, honestly, respectfully and directly.

- We are fully present.

- We are all accountable.

- We trust and assume goodness in intentions.

- We are continuous learners."[64]

Okay, now you might not know this about me if you have read my books or attended my presentations, but I aspire to live my life in accordance with these guiding behaviors. I was told that they are aspirational behaviors not prescriptive. In other words, the culture recognizes that no one is perfect and yet we are all expected to aspire to these behaviors and to remind others to do so while reinforcing the behaviors through feedback.

---

[63]Source: https://www.trinity-health.org/about-us/mission-core-values-and-vision
[64] *Source:* https://jobs.trinity-health.org/stjoes/why-us

Before continuing, I think I should note that while this was a not-for-profit, faith-based organization it was more non-denominational. If you look at these guiding principles and what they represent, it is more about getting the organization to work toward common goals and behave in a manner that is respectful and collaborative. It is one thing to put platitudes on the wall, and quite another to explain exactly what the behaviors that support that goal look like on a day-to-day, moment-by-moment basis.

I included the information on this remarkable culture for four reasons:

1. This approach to culture demonstrates the power of culture. It is said when an individual squares off against the culture, the culture always wins; I think of *One Flew Over the Cuckoo's Nest* when I hear this. Even though the protagonist, Randall Patrick McMurphy, tries to buck the culture by violating every rule in the book, the organization pushes back...hard. In the end he is lobotomized, and while the Big Chief escaped to freedom, several patients lost their lives. Others left the hospital, but the core culture of the hospital remained the same or at very least very rapidly returned to its former state.

2. By codifying the connection between the mission through the vision and concluding with guiding behaviors, you can profoundly influence the climate of an organization. I haven't worked in this culture in over a decade and yet the guiding principles stay with me. We didn't just talk about these things—we lived them. When I was there, the first year turnover rate was very high—far higher than any organization would find acceptable, but those who made it through the first year tended to have an average tenure in the double digits; not bad for an organization that had only existed for 20 odd years.

3. To remind you of the importance of speaking up. The guiding principles have evolved and morphed over the years (owing largely to mergers and acquisitions) but when I was there the guiding principles contained something about ministering to the body, mind, and spirit and bits

about social justice. This was a culture where people were expected to speak up. Standing idly on the sidelines of life was not tolerated. It felt good to be on the side of justice

4. Finally, and most importantly, the company policies reflected all of the guiding principles. There was a policy that made threatening, or even JOKING about, violence grounds for termination. It got a bit ridiculous because we weren't allowed to call bullets well...bullets, even though the term "bullet" predates the invention of ammunition or firearms.

5. We can't ever underestimate the power that words have and how language can either reinforce the desired culture or undermine it. I write everything I write with this in mind. As I mentioned previously, we can't change someone's mind without by-passing the walls they threw up using the logical part of their brains. Words are a shortcut to the emotional part of the brain and it is important that we choose them wisely.

Just one last thought on culture: why is it that so many people willingly accept that a cult can grow up rapidly and become deeply entrenched, and yet the same people believe creating a corporate culture that addresses and discourages violence is impossible?

Summary

While it is true that rampage killers are ultimately responsible for their actions and must always be accountable, it is also true that the triggers of a rampage killer are often environmental. By controlling the culture of a workplace, one can diminish many of the most common antecedents to a rampage killer event. The most dangerous cultures are the Dating Game Culture, The Tyrant Culture, the Frat House Culture, and the Pressure Cooker, and when you recognize your work environment in one or more of these cultures you need to intervene and more than likely you will need a trained and skilled consultant to assist you in making this change.

Thought Starters

Changing from a toxic culture to a culture of resilience is difficult. Why do you think that it is so hard to make these changes?

Once you recognize that the shadow of a leader is toxic, how would you go about addressing this?

What is the first step in eliminating peer-to-peer bullying?

To a large extent bullying is in the eye of the beholder. What one person sees as a harmless letting off steam another may see as bullying. How can you tell the difference?

How has broadening the definition of "bullying" impacted the view of the problem?

Stop. Don't Shoot!

Chapter 12: Going Postal

In the early 90s there began a spate of workplace rampage attacks among U.S. Postal Service workers that came to be known as "going postal." The term is revealing because it provides us with a glimpse inside of the mind of a rampage killer. But what's the difference between a single shooter event and "going postal?" In his book *Beyond Going Postal: Shifting from Workplace Tragedies and Toxic Work Environment to Safe and Healthy Organization*, Dr. Steve Musacco explains that, "Many people have asked: Why is there so much stress and workplace tragedies in the U.S. Postal Service? The answer to these questions is because the postal culture embraces and reflects core values that center on achieving bottom-line results with little or no regard for employee participation, respect, dignity, or fairness. Additionally, there is little or no accountability for the actions of top management in the Postal Service. Many postal facilities consequently have toxic work environments, and they can be a catalyst or trigger for serious acts of workplace violence, including homicide and suicide. The associated rewards system for behavior consistent with the postal culture core values, moreover, enables systemic organizational and individual bullying of employees at all levels of the organization."[65]

Dr. Musacco was not alone in his beliefs, and other studies portrayed the post office as a quasi-military operation that used many of the same tactics as the military. These tactics, while arguably appropriate in the military (I have learned that there are some people that will argue endlessly over anything,) where the goal is to create soldiers who follow orders without questioning them, is completely inappropriate in a civilian workplace. Think about it: training military personnel means indoctrinating them into a mindset where their own personal safety is less important than completing the mission. It's messy for us civilians to think about training young men and women to be prepared to sacrifice their very lives in the furtherance of a plan that they don't understand; but that is what they must do.

For years the U.S. Air Force was hailed as having the best training in the country, if not the world, and many companies sought to emulate this training. I agree the training is excellent for its intended purpose, but I disagree that it should be used in the civilian world. It's hard to imagine that postal workers should be expected to die so that the mail gets delivered. Many people erroneously believe that postal carriers take the oath "Neither snow, nor rain, nor heat, nor gloom of night stays these couriers from the swift completion of their appointed rounds." While this is not now, and has never been in any way associated with the U.S. Postal service, it speaks to the high standards set by the service and the postal workers themselves.[66]

Unfortunately managing postal carriers in the same way you would military personnel sent many workers to the breaking point. The point is that going postal was the result of a uniquely toxic work culture that the United States Postal Service has since taken steps to correct. In fact, the last postal attack was on December 23, 2017, where a postal worker beat the postmaster to death over his

---

[65] *Source: Beyond Going Postal: Shifting from Workplace Tragedies and Toxic Work Environment to Safe and Healthy Organization, January 27, 2009*
[66] *Source: https://about.usps.com/who/profile/history/pdf/mission-motto.pdf*

pending dismissal. This was the first fatal workplace violence event in the US Postal Service since 2006.[67] This latest case puts the United States Postal Service on a par with most any other workplace.

As far-fetched as it seems, I was physically present at two of the first rampage attacks. The first rampage attack (at which I was present) was in Royal Oak, Michigan. My boss and I were headed to downtown Royal Oak when I asked him to swing by the post office so that I could mail a bill. He asked if I had to go in and I told him I did because I needed a stamp. My boss responded that he thought he might have a stamp. He looked in his wallet and said, "It is YOUR lucky day!"as he proudly produced his last stamp. I put the stamp on the envelope and we put it in the mailbox out front. Just then we heard sirens screaming from all directions as we continued to a restaurant. It was hours later that I learned how close I came to being right in the middle of the carnage, and maybe even being killed.

The second incident at which I was present was at the Dearborn, Michigan Post Office. I got lost and didn't have a cell phone. I tried to pull into the Post Office parking lot and was stopped by a police officer. I told him I just needed to use the pay phone and he said, "You don't want to go in there; people are dying in there." I don't mind telling you that I was shaken up. But for a few minutes (the gunman was still alive and shooting) I could well have been injured or killed.

I should point out that a lot of people have a lot of levity about the number of close calls I have had with the Angel of Death and the sheer number of people that I know personally who have died in industrial accidents, but I tell them that I don't get hired by companies who are performing at optimal levels (some are, but most need me to take care of a specific problem or set of problems.) It could also be that I don't have the sense that God gave geese, but I try not to think about it.

---

[67]*Source: Beyond Going Postal: Shifting from Workplace Tragedies and Toxic Work Environment to Safe and Healthy Organization, January 27, 2009*

The fact that these two early attacks were in metropolitan Detroit is also telling. In its heyday, Detroit was a boomtown. My late father used to tell the tale of coming home from the service at the end of World War II. He got a job working at the Ford Motor Company but he didn't like it, so he quit at lunch and walked across the street where he got a job at Firestone. He didn't like working at Firestone either, so the next day he took a job at Detroit Edison where he worked for over 40 years before retiring.

Despite this boom, Detroit was taken down in the 70s by the oil embargo (with its unprecedented spike in gasoline prices and shortages) and fuel efficient Japanese-manufactured vehicles. Prior to the success of companies like Toyota, Honda, and Mitsubishi the phrase "Made in Japan" was synonymous with cheap, poorly-made goods. But moving to light-weight, fuel efficient vehicles, while difficult for "The Big Three"[68] was a relatively simple endeavor for Japanese manufacturers. Part of the terms of surrender by the Japanese was that they were forbidden from making vehicles of war. An unintended outcome of this was a switch from making planes to manufacturing motorcycles and light-weight cars. The treaty was only one factor in the equation, Japan's densely populated cities and heavy traffic didn't lend itself to the big, heavy, fuel gobblers that were popular in the U.S. when the oil embargo hit.

Another factor in Detroit's downfall was the relatively poor quality of it's vehicles[69]—the rapid move to light-weight vehicles adversely impacted the sketchy quality of its products. Eiji Toyoda[70] visited the Ford Rouge plant in Detroit. The plant once was the pinnacle of Henry Ford's genius with rubber, silica, and other raw materials delivered at one end of the complex and new cars rolling off the assembly line at the other. Toyoda made multiple trips to the Rouge complex and learned much, most of it

---

[68] *A term many, especially the media, used to describe General Motors, Ford, and Chrysler*
[69] *I speak from first-hand experience. My first car was an absolute steaming pile of pig excrement, a 1976 Ford Granada. I used to joke that it was my girlfriend because it never wanted to go where I wanted to go. I spent all my money on it, and every chance it got it screwed me.*
[70] *He named the company that he would eventually found "Toyota" because he felt that giving the company his family name was ostentatious.*

about eliminating waste and improving quality by tapping into the vast resource of the worker's knowledge.[71] The reality of dropping out of high school and getting a high-paying job "working the line" was shattered forever. So many people were leaving Michigan that the saying "would the last person leaving Michigan please turn out the lights" became popular. There were no jobs for people without a college education and even those with degrees were challenged by the job shortages. If you didn't have a stellar pedigree you couldn't expect to find a job, or at least a job that paid a living wage.

Except for working at the Post Office. All one needed to do was pass the civil service exam and apply. Getting a job at the Post Office didn't require a ridiculously lengthy Curriculum Vitae to get a job. The pay was great, the benefits obscene, and the work—while often physically demanding—was a walk in the park compared to factory work (I worked for several years at the General Motors Fleetwood Plant–I screwed for a living and came home sore and still have scarred corneas from the metal slivers that blew into my eyes. I literally felt like crying driving home on Fridays thinking about going back on Monday.) For the unemployed and people like me, working at the Post Office was a dream come true. And so things played out all over America as Reagan's trickle down policies didn't quite trickle far enough, but that is fodder for another book.

The confluence of achieving an ideal job and idyllic benefits that required little or no advanced education in an economy so bad that the U.S. military was turning away eager recruits, with a quasi-military, some might say sadistic and toxic work environment created the perfect breeding ground for a person to snap and kill. So while today's rampage killers might be the product of a toxic workplace, the motivations of these rampaging killers is not the same as those tragic cases where a person, pushed to the edge and threatened with losing a job that they could not reasonably expect to ever replicate.

[71]*Source: The Machine that Changed World: the story of Lean Production How Japan's Secret Weapon in the Global Auto Wars Will Revolutionize Western Industry James P. Womack, Daniel T. Jones, and Daniel Roos HarperCollins Publishing, New York, 1991*

Summary

Rampage attacks at the U.S. Postal Service were an alarming phenomenon caused by systemic bullying coupled with a poor economy that forever transitioned away from high paying factory jobs which required no college (and often not even a high school diploma) toward a service economy where the jobs paid significantly less and required at least some college. Postal workers suffered the bullying because they knew that if they quit, they would never have it that good again until finally the stress grew to intolerable proportions. Much work has been done to dismantle this institutional abuse of power, and now the USPS is no more likely to have a rampage attack than any other industry.

Thought Starters

What lessons can we learn from the rampage attacks that occurred at the USPS?

What should a job applicant look for in a corporate culture before accepting a job offer?

Since the USPS was able to make such significant changes in such a large organization in a relatively short time, why do you think it is so difficult for other organizations to do so?

Stop. Don't Shoot!

Chapter 13: Creating A Culture Of Resilience

R esilience is all the rage right now, and for good reason. For one, it is backed by a wide body of research and excellent books that are easy to read and understand. A good portion of resilience is focusing on reducing stress (as we will discuss), how we manage our stress individually, AND how we look to decrease unnecessary stress in our corporate cultures.

In a cultural sense, resilience is an individual's or a culture's ability to rebound after setbacks—whether it be a poor performance evaluation or a tragedy in the workplace. Resilience is more than just the latest Human Resource buzzword—resilient people tend to stay healthy, have fewer workplace injuries, recover from sickness faster when they do get ill, lose their tempers less frequently, and live happier, more peaceful, and low-stress lives. And most importantly in the context of this book, the resilient person is far less likely to snap and go on a rampage attack.

Even the friendliest parents will tell their children not to talk to strangers. Why? Aren't strangers just friends we haven't met yet? We warn our children about strangers because of a potential threat, not an actual threat. Our brains treat the nonverbal, subconscious input in the exact same way. When in doubt, sound the alarm. The brain figures that it's better to have chemicals that we don't need than it is to need chemicals that we don't have; but this is not necessarily a healthy outlook. What's worse is that because our brains respond to the absence of information in the same way they do to real danger indicators. Our brains must assume that information that is not in the danger database is a threat; if it assumes a perception is benign when it is malignant, the body is completely vulnerable. But if the brain assumes the perception is malignant when it is actually benign, the body is still ready for action and assumes no real risk. A lack of information from an authority figure will lead to paranoia. If our bosses don't talk to us, we convince ourselves that our boss doesn't like us. If the silence continues, we may convince ourselves that our boss intends to fire us. Left unchecked, this fear may make us dislike our boss to the point where we quit or act out and get fired.

All of this hardwired, instinctual behavior makes us less resilient and all of the benefits of being resilient are replaced with opposite effects. Creating a resilient workplace becomes essential. To complicate matters, non-verbal warnings may not even come from our own senses, often we are victims of "herd stress." Herd stress is a situation created when an individual picks up the stress of his or her surroundings. Watch a documentary on the animals of Africa and you will likely see an excellent example of herd stress.

A herd of gazelles stands leisurely grazing. Suddenly one tenses at a hint of danger. Within seconds, the whole herd is on full alert and in the blink of an eye the herd stampedes as one, out of harm's way. Are we humans so different? When we pick up nonverbal cues that indicate that someone around us is stressed, we become stressed. Why? Because our brains sense that even though it can detect no danger, perhaps someone else in the tribe has perceived danger. Our bodies will react without waiting to see if the threat is real. Think of this as the "lookout reflex." Our bodies rely on "look outs" to warn them of dangers that we either have not detected or have not yet cataloged as dangers.

Imagine our senses as our bodies' radar. We gather information about our physical environment and scan for dangers. If our senses pick up no sign of danger, we are completely relaxed. If, on the other hand, our bodies detect potential dangers, they put our bodies on alert; the level of alertness corresponds to the level of the perceived danger.

The United States military uses a system to rate security threats on a five-point scale. Defcon 5 represents the lowest level of threat, while Defcon 1 represents the highest. This is an apt analogy for our bodies' system for evaluating danger. When we are relaxing and having fun, our internal radar has sensed no threats and so it offers no reaction, it's at Defcon 5. But as the subconscious mind identifies potential threats, it moves us to a more heightened state, Defcon 4. If the threats need to be monitored but prove no immediate threat, Defcon 3. If the threats are more serious, and so on. Anything that interferes with our ability to correctly monitor the dangers around us causes de facto stress. Listening to music so loud that we can't hear an ambulance siren is very stressful, for example. Our internal radar is jammed so we must drop to Defcon 3, since that is the only way our subconscious can be sure that we are protected. Great! So we have to sit around in silence or stress will kill us, right? Well, silence can also stress us. Nature teems with noises, from crickets chirping to birds singing. Silence in the forest usually signals a danger is looming. The last thing one hears before the leopard attacks is an unnerving silence before the roar.[72]

By surrounding yourself with silence, you may be adding to your stress. Our bodies need and expect to hear some ambient noise; without some noise our radar may believe the senses are malfunctioning, or that the lack of noise is just the silence before the roar. Remember, our brains didn't construct the danger database in a vacuum, rather it assigned meaning to each of the inputs it received.

The popularity of recordings of natural sounds (waves crashing, wolves howling, rain falling) is testament to the soothing effects of

---

[72]*Having never been killed by a leopard, I can only speculate on this.*

nature. So much of the information we receive is non-verbal and subconscious that sometimes we see some "unexplained" phenomena, like psychic flashes and premonitions. Have you ever had a dream that foretold the future? Predicted the death of a loved one? While there are cases where such phenomena cannot be readily dismissed, in many cases these psychic emanations are nothing more mysterious than our subconscious mind reading clues that our conscious minds miss and predicting a likely outcome. Take the psychic flash that foretells the death of someone you know. Isn't it plausible that your internal radar picked up nonverbal cues from the person (subtle changes in skin color, behavior, tone of voice, weight, etc,) that gave your subconscious a clue that all was not well with the person's physical or mental condition, even though the person may not have been aware of his or her own weakening physical state or decreased judgment?

Why Worry: Stress that We Deliberately Create

Another common source of stress is what I call "predictive stress." Predictive stress arises from the common practice of trying to relieve the pressures of worrying by asking "What's the worst thing that could happen?" Asking this question is incredibly stress producing, as we now add a whole list of calamities to our worries.

Often we tend to catastrophize: we turn an everyday stressor into an armageddon. It's not bad enough that we worried that our boss didn't like us, now well-meaning but dim-witted friends introduce the worst- case scenario and we add being fired, losing our homes, and becoming destitute and diseased homeless nomads driven mad by life's luxuries lost. Gee, that's a cheery thought, thank you for adding to my gloom. It makes sense that if we don't have a complete picture of a situation that we would have to prepare for the worst-case scenario. The problem with this practice is that the worst-case scenario is seldom the mostly likely scenario. Instead of picturing the worst-case scenario, we should picture, and plan for, the most likely scenario. When we plan for the most likely scenario, it's prudent to prepare some contingency plans (saving money for a rainy day, for example) but we need to stop our armageddon thinking and concentrate on real issues and the actions we can take to minimize our risks and to mitigate the damage from an undesired outcome.

Take for instance the prospect of losing your job. Economic conditions, management decisions, and a host of other factors that could contribute to losing our jobs are completely beyond our control, so worrying about these and obsessing about them is a complete waste of time: the stress consumes our energy, making us less resilient and providing us with nothing of value in return. Resiliency efforts seek to provide tools to teach people to see opportunities and silver linings. For example, a highly resilient person doesn't waste energy worrying about losing his or her job. Instead of worrying about the prospect of losing a job, we need to make contingency plans and take action. For example, as I write this my job hangs by a thread. What can I do? Well, for starters, I can take control of my life and get my resumé and CV in order, I can let my network know of the uncertain employment situation, and I can start applying for other jobs. In other words I can do something constructive—even if my efforts bear no fruit, I can focus on mitigating the damage instead of stewing about impending doom.

In all the toxic environments we discussed before, there is a common denominator: high stress and an acceptance of abhorrent behavior. A resilient culture is marked by:

- **Compassion.** a binary "right/wrong" view of behavior and communicate openly and honestly with workers to determine the causes of undesirable behaviors before deciding on a course of action. Human error—irrespective of the outcome—is consoled. Take for example the case where a nurse accidentally gave adult doses of a medicine to newborns. Several infants died. A complete investigation found that the adult and infant medications were stored side by side in nearly identical packaging (the only difference was small Organizations that are highly resilient encourage compassionate management. These organizations don't have print indicating whether it was for adults or infants.) Virtually anyone could have made this same mistake, and the system had so many poor designs that failure was all but certain. If it wasn't this nurse who made the mistake, someone else would eventually have done the same thing. So what is the compassionate response? Console the nurse and reassure her (in this case) that the deaths, while a result of her error, were all but unavoidable. The hospital took immediate action to work with the manufacturer to design noticeably different packaging and to segregate adult medications (of all kinds) from pediatric medication.

Compassion extends far beyond forgiving human error, and includes policies that go beyond regulatory requirements for family leave or similar situations. A resilient culture provides resources for things like elder or childcare, or unlimited sick and bereavement leave. There are even forward-thinking companies that offer paid "mental-wellness" leave. I have worked in several companies that had formal bereavement policies that were enforced compassionately. When my mother died, the owner of the company not only sent flowers and came to the funeral, but he also told me not to worry about what the policy said, but for me to take as much time as I needed. Similarly, while working at another job, my father died and again, not only did the owner of the company attend the services at the funeral home AND the funeral, but so did all of the company's executives, AND my teammates. It was very touching to me because the trip for many of them was 50 miles or more one way, and I had only been on the job for less than eight months. Still another employer insisted that I take more time off when my brother-in-law died, and even though I didn't feel I needed it, it helped me grieve. In all these cases, the compassion demonstrated by my managers, executives, and colleagues made me feel more comfortable, loyal, and more aligned with the company's values.

If you want to create a culture of resilience, review your policies and ask yourself if they were borne of compassion or designed to protect the company from liars, cheats, and malingerers. If you treat your employees as if they are liars, cheats, and malingerers, they will become just that. That statement has some of you freaking out. Who will come to work if we provide unlimited paid sick or bereavement leave?!?!?! I once worked at a company that had a very simple sick leave policy: if you're sick, stay home.[73] The average sick leave taken as a company of 6,000 was .5 hours per employee per year. When managers complained that there was no sick leave policy, Human Resources acquiesced and each employee was allotted 5 sick days per year. Within six months, the sick leave usage had risen to an average of 4.5 days a year. Was anything accomplished in doing this? Or was the company better off with its previous, more compassionate, approach?

There is a great book that relates to this topic, *Raving Fans: A Revolutionary Approach to Customer Service* by Ken Blanchard and Sheldon Bowles. The book demonstrates many of the characteristics of a resilient culture, but that is not its intent. I cite it just for all you uptight managers who mistake compassion for weakness. In the book, a character goes into a department store and is shocked to learn that he can take as much merchandise into the changing room as he wants. He questions the manager, asking incredulously if the store was unconcerned about theft. The manager laughed and said that they have found that only a small percent of their customers are likely to steal, and it seemed downright insulting to treat 99% of the customers as potential thieves when only 1% stole.Expect greatness from your workers and they will seldom disappoint you. Very few will cheat the system, so manage those few who do. In his book *Resilient: How To Grow An Unshakable Calm, Strength, And Happiness*, Rick Hanson, Ph.D, defines compassion as "warm-hearted concern for suffering and the desire to relieve it if you can" and further adds

---

[73]*A manager was always within his or her rights to ask for a doctor's excuse, but encouraged to do so only if he or she was worried about the worker's health.*

"Compassion is a psychological resource—an inner strength— that can be developed over time." As you review your policies, ask yourself what your company is doing to build your workforce's psychological resources.

- Mindfulness. Hanson identifies mindfulness as the second element of resilience. In short, mindfulness is the practice of focusing your mind on positives, and training yourself to overcome the natural tendency to be pessimistic. I have started many presentations asking the simple question: why don't we let our children take candy from strangers? The answer is simple pragmatism and risk to reward ratio. Four possible conditions exist:

    1. A stranger wants to harm our child and succeeds.

    2. A stranger wants to harm our child and does not succeed.

    3. A stranger does not want to harm our child and gives them a harmless treat.

    4. A stranger does not want to harm our child and our child does not engage with the stranger.

In all of these scenarios, a stranger could easily harm our child. By telling our children to avoid strangers, we are able to avoid a horrendous outcome. So, despite the fact that most strangers are not trying to harm our children, we chose to allow our suspicions to guide our behavior. This pessimism is more than just a defense mechanism against disappointment—it actually creates physiological pathways that make us less resilient. I am not recommending that you encourage your children to take candy from strangers (unless the candy is exceptionally good and expensive.[74]) Do I really have to tell you that I am not recommending that children take candy from strangers? But you should encourage your children to avoid putting themselves at risk and that there are people (both strangers and people known to

---

[74]*NEVER take parenting advice from me.*

them) who may try to hurt them. It is a delicate balance between keeping your children safe and terrifying them. Remember here the stress of always being alert to dangers; people tend to see the fight/flight response as a binary response (we either rapidly react to danger in one of these ways or we don't) but we know intuitively that most strangers don't want to hurt our children. And yet, as the spate of school rampage attacks demonstrates, there are enough strangers who want to hurt our children that it is beyond prudent to teach your children how to reduce their risk and to mitigate the most likely harm.

- **Continual Learning.** Learning helps us overcome our natural tendency to expect and prepare for disaster. Amazingly, learning doesn't just provide us new knowledge or skills, but it also improves our neural pathways and allows us to build the skills we need to see the silver lining in situations instead of the potential dangers. Optimism is a skill that needs to be learned, but before you can learn to be optimistic, you have to unlearn the default setting of pessimism that our subconscious has programmed for us. Abraham Lincoln reputedly said (and this is in dispute by pedantic mouth-breathers with nothing better to do) "We're just about as happy as we make up our minds to be." As it turns out, it appears that not only was Abe right on this account, but his quote is backed up by hard science.

- **Resources to Build Physical Strength**. Fitness centers in businesses were popular in the late 1980s and early 1990s, but companies, citing the cost of maintaining facilities and the lack of use by workers, phased these programs out. Today, programs designed to improve workers' physical fitness are making a rebound. Scientists are finding that working out not only improves your immune system and helps prevent or stave off adverse medical conditions, but will actually make you happier and therefore more resilient.

- **Stress Management.** Stress management will always be a hot topic. Stress, simply put, is our body's way of protecting us from danger. Without stress, we would blissfully roast our hands against a hot stove, or lop our way into oncoming traffic where smiling motorists would mow us down. We owe our lives to stress. When stress is properly applied to our bodies, it saves our lives. We yank our hands away from hot stoves, leap in panicked jerks out of the path of oncoming traffic as the freaked-out motorist careens wildly through the lanes to avoid us. Yes, stress is an important part of our survival. But what about when stress is misused, misinterpreted, or misdirected by our bodies? (did I miss any "misses?") The same reflexes designed to preserve our fleshy behinds turn on our bodies like a jilted ex-lover. Most of the information our brains receive comes to us through our subconscious. In order for us to be able to focus and concentrate on abstract tasks, our brains automate many of our routine tasks. Picture your brain as a computer filled with thousands of software programs that automate the simpler tasks, and even some tasks that are not so simple. How many of us have to stop and think about the physical steps required to turn a doorknob, start a car, or drive to work? We do all these things without thinking because our brain has automated these tasks.

The old joke about not being able to walk and chew gum at the same time is funny precisely because our brains have so automated these tasks that to not be able to do both at the time is ludicrous. While the conscious mind doesn't bother with the mundane, the subconscious works overtime to get us through our day. In addition to running these "subroutines," our brains must sort through the tons of information that they receive. Our brains then route some of the information to our conscious minds while filing most of it away in our subconscious, where it is compared by the nervous system against our "database of danger." Forgive my melodrama, but I think the analogy is an apt one. As infants, we come into this world with very little information; we're helpless. Through a concerted effort on the part of our brains, we gather as much information as we can as quickly as we can. We soon learn that a hot stove is far too dangerous to be trifled with and so we file away in our subconscious any inputs—visual, aural, oral, tactile, and olfactory—that are even remotely related to the danger we call a hot stove. Our subconscious even writes a program that causes us to remove our hand from a hot stove so fast that we have removed ourselves from the danger before our conscious minds even realize what's happening. Our subconscious has saved us using what scientists call the fight-flight reflex.[75]

The fight-flight response is our bodies' way of protecting us from all the dangers that we have filed away in the "danger database." As we are bombarded with information, our brains sift through the small percentage that is necessary for our cognitive functions, or in other words the things that require us to think, for instance, reading. Do you find it difficult to concentrate in a room filled with noise? Is it more difficult for you to read when surrounded by a flurry of activity? If so, the difficulty likely arises from your brain trying to sort through the input to determine whether or not a danger is present. In the time you are taking to read this, your brain is being deluged with sensory input. Perhaps a fluorescent light is buzzing nearby, or maybe a television plays off in the distance. While you aren't conscious of the input, your subconscious is carefully and quickly reviewing the information and checking it against your danger database.

The term has evolved to Fight-Flight-Freeze, but I see Flight and Freeze as essentially the same response, we either adopt an aggressive stance or a passive/defensive stance. In most cases these inputs are harmless and your

---

[75] *I think it's important that in the age of "seen it on the internet" (sung to the tune of Marvin Gaye's "Heard It The Grapevine") some people dispute the mechanics I just described; but the disputes are nit picking. These people would write an article on the Hindenberg's maiden voyage by focusing on how cramped the seats were and how little space there was for luggage, completely missing the explosion.*

subconscious doesn't bother you with them. In some cases, these inputs match a danger in the database and trigger a conscious response. In still other cases, the input doesn't provide enough information for a definitive conclusion to be made and the brain has to assume a "better safe than sorry" posture. In these cases, the brain prepares the body for the worst-case scenario and the result is stress.

Just as touching a hand to a hot stove elicits a rapid response where we jerk our hand from harm's way, so too does our body react to subtler threats (although in far less dramatic ways.) Whenever our bodies perceive danger, our brains activate the "flight or fight" reflex. First, our bodies give us an energy rush as they release stored sugar and fats into the bloodstream. Next, our brains increase our breathing to supply more oxygen to the blood—oxygen that will be needed to give our bodies the short-term boost needed to combat the danger. Our heart rate then accelerates to provide more blood to the muscles. Newly flush with more blood, our muscles tense for action. Blood is also routed to the brain and away from the stomach and digestion stops. Our senses become more acute and actively scan for more signs of danger. Finally, alertness heightens to the point where it becomes difficult to focus. Our bodies turn into finely honed killing machines ready to strike down danger in its tracks.

Unfortunately, not all triggers are, in fact, dangers. Most of us have heard of mothers who experience brief moments of superhuman strength and lift a car off a trapped child, a testament (whether factual or not) to the benefits of the fight-flight reflex. But what about instances where the threat isn't real? What effect does the fight-flight reflex have in imagined or misperceived threats? The body reacts to a threat that isn't there the same way it does to real threats, it gets ready to bust a head or bust a move. In the cases where the threat is imaginary, or chronic, our brains flood our bodies with toxic chemicals that we don't really need and can't use, and so our bodies are left to deal with these chemicals the same way it deals with other poisons.

Remember the story of the Sword of Damocles? In this legend, Damocles expresses his envy for the life of a king he was visiting, marveling at the luxurious palace, array of servants, and beautiful women at the king's disposal. To prove a point (to put it mildly) the king orders his servants to suspend a sword above Damocles' head with a single string (more than kind of a dick move, if you ask me). The king then tells Damocles that this is what the king's life is like; always wondering if the string will break and he will be killed. For many of us, our lives are like the Sword of Damocles, and our bodies react to the stress of wondering when the dangers we continuously perceive will make their moves and force us into action.

Stress is designed to protect us, so why does it cause us harm? The fight-flight reflex was designed as a short-term solution to an acute, life-threatening situation, by kicking our bodies into overdrive, but the bulb that burns twice as bright burns half as long. Instead of releasing a massive dose of chemicals, we instead release low-level doses of toxins that wear out our bodies. When our fight-flight reflex is activated, our brains become miniature chemical plants as an area of the brain stem releases of a variety of chemicals:

Norepinephrine is a hormone that in turn causes the Adrenal glands to release and pump out Adrenaline. Adrenaline increases our heart rate and raises our metabolism, and in anticipation our hearts beat faster, our blood pressure increases, our pulses race causing us to sweat and to breath heavily. This "shot of adrenaline" is critical to our survival, but this barrage of chemicals affects our emotions and leaves us feeling anxious, worried, and even paranoid—even when the danger isn't real. We tend to think of the fight-flight reflex as an all or nothing proposition, but is it? What about small dangers that we encounter that don't escalate into a full-blown crisis? In these cases, the brain still releases chemicals and prepares our bodies for battle. Blood is rerouted, smaller amounts of chemicals are released; instead of an immediate response the brain gradually puts us on alert, changing our body chemistry and putting a long-term stress on our major biological systems.

Let's again take a look at what is happening to our bodies: our heart rate increases. An accelerated heartrate is useful in a crisis, but a chronic increase leads to high blood pressure. We breathe faster, providing more oxygen, but when the condition is chronic it causes chest pains from a tired, strained diaphragm. Digestion stops as blood leaves the stomach; this causes a variety of digestive problems and aggravates ulcers. Blood leaves the hands, head, and feet, which causes headaches and cold hands and feet. Coagulation of the blood increases, which increases the likelihood of blood clots and strokes. Muscles tense in anticipation of an attack which leads to chronic muscle pain and fatigue.

In short, if we expose ourselves to low-grade stresses, we use our body in a way in which it was never intended and it wears our. Just as a building that was designed to withstand a great force all at once will gradually fall apart from years of light wear, so too will our bodies fall apart from constant exposure to stress.

Some of you may be thinking, "Okay, this makes sense, but I don't exactly have a whole lot of danger in my life. But I still have a whole lot of stress." I doubt any of us have no dangers around us, although I grant you most of the dangers that our bodies perceive aren't real. Again, most communication is nonverbal, in other words, most information we gather about our surroundings comes from our senses, and not from what we read or what is spoken to us. Our senses are barraged with input that our brain sorts and filters and assigns a level of importance. We need only take a moment, close our eyes, and listen to the noises in the room. How many previously unnoticed noises do you hear? All our senses are gathering data at a blinding speed and storing it in the wonderful and amazing database of our brain. Some of these inputs the brain decides are worthy of the attention of the conscious mind while others it stores in our subconscious mind for later retrieval and use if necessary.

The brain rightfully judges much of the input from our senses as benign, while other information is matched up against our database to see if it is indicative of danger. If one smells smoke, one is likely to investigate the cause. Why? Is the smell of smoke so unpleasant that we should immediately eradicate it?No. Why then do we investigate the smell of smoke? To be sure there is no danger of fire.

So what does any of this have to do with stress? As infants, we gather and catalog sensory input. Some of these inputs we categorize as harmless and others we categorize as harmful. We are confronted with many things we've programmed ourselves to see as potential hazards every day. Take for instance the baby crying on an airplane. We know that babies cry for a variety of reasons that have nothing to do with any sort of danger to us, yet the baby's cry produces physiological responses in our body because our subconscious catalog equates crying with danger.

In many cases, our poor brains don't have enough information to make an informed decision as to whether or not to sound the alarms, so it assumes the worst. In the early days of humanity mankind didn't have the luxury of mistakes, if Grog ate the blue food and died, the rest of the tribe steered clear of blue food, reasoning it was better to miss out on a culinary delight that it is to die an agonizing death from ingesting poison. The idea that what you don't know can kill you is hardwired into our brains, and the human-animal has adapted to this such that if we don't have enough information, we fill in the gaps with the worst case scenario.

Superstitions grew out of man's need to accurately predict the outcome of serious situations, like a major battle or the harvest crops. Desperate to predict the future, man turned to oracles, mystics, and fortune tellers. Primitive societies didn't have a whole lot of stress as we know it, but they had their fair share of death.

The optimists among us are now shaking their heads and decrying this as heresy, but consider this situation: your boss tells everyone in the department (except you) that they are to be in a mandatory meeting at 9:00 a.m. the next morning. When you ask your boss if you need to be there, your boss says, "No, I just need to see everyone else." You ask similarly tight-lipped co-workers who tell you they "aren't allowed to talk about the meeting, or what it's about."

Now, you ask yourself, is the purpose of the meeting to plan a surprise party for you, or is some sinister plot afoot? Is this example really so absurd? What responsible parent tells a child "if a stranger offers you a ride, you take it. You never know when another stranger will be by and the next stranger may not offer!" With all that in mind, let's take a look at the characteristics of a resilient culture:

- **Fun**. Resilient cultures are fun places to work. Work and fun are not mutually exclusive. People who have fun at work, celebrate successes, and have a sense of humor are more resilient than those who do not.[76]

- **Social Support**. Resilient cultures openly encourage the celebrations of life's great moments and love and support in times of tragedy. These activities are voluntary and organic, not mandatory. A friend of mine used to work for a company that tried to force teamwork and a social support network by having mandatory and unpaid weekend canoe trips. She hated canoeing and didn't much care for her coworkers. She didn't go, and was docked on her performance review for missing it. This is so incredibly stupid I don't even have a comment or a joke. The story itself is more sad and Kafkaesque than I could ever make it. It is so ludicrous that even I, the king of tall tales, lacks the imagination to make it up. Social support networks are most effective when they are organic and the way to create an organic social support system, as contradictory as that sounds, is to create an environment that is supportive and conducive for workers to be there for one another.

Summary

Resilience is a term that describes how quickly and effectively a person recovers from trauma. People with a high degree of resilience are able to recover from emotional and physical trauma much more quickly than those people with less resilience. Resilient cultures tend to have institutionalized tools for encouraging people to build relationships and social support networks.

Resilient cultures and positive work environments help prevent rampage attacks because mentally unstable individuals are given the care and support that they need. Potential targets are supported

---

[76] *So people who have complained about my use of humor during my speeches and presentations and in my writing can suck it—I'm not unprofessional, I'm resilient.*

by a network of caring coworkers who can both steer them towards the resources that they need and can watch out for the security of the potential target, and more importantly the resilient environment provides both the unstable loner and the potential target a legitimately caring environment and reduces the risk of workplace violence.

Thought Starters

Why is a resilient workplace (and resilient workers) important?

How can a company justify the cost of employee resiliency programs?

Why is a resilient culture safer than a non- or low-resilience organization?

How can you spot the signals that a worker is under continual stress, and when should you intervene? How?

Stop. Don't Shoot!

Chapter 14: Surviving a Rampage Attack

Whether or not your employees survive a rampage attack relies on your ability to spot red flags—both in people and in your location. Rampage attacks can happen anywhere, but some of the most likely areas are the workplace, venues that attract large crowds, and soft targets (like schools.) The time to think about surviving a rampage attack is long before the event occurs. You should know precisely what to do before an event occurs. "In my experience, most shooters have a target in mind when they arrive on scene. Others are victims of opportunity or collateral damage. Shooter gets on a roll! Some may try to intervene or are seen as being "sympathetic" to the initial victim." says Andrew Arena.

So what does preparation look like?

- Preparing for surviving a rampage attack begins with your situational awareness, meaning that you need to be cognizant of your surroundings and indications of things that might seem out of place or dangerous.

- Position yourself to have clear access to an exit.

- If you cannot escape, find cover.

During the Attack

Forget the "run, hide, fight back" method, it has shown to be ineffective. Let's look at why:

- **Run.** People are predators, and the eyes of predators are attracted to sudden, panicked movements. Instead of safety, walk quickly to an exit or a predetermined hiding place. If it is too late to do this, fall to the floor and stay motionless. Running to a hiding place may well lead the attacker to a target rich environment, you will get yourself killed and likely a lot of other innocent people as well.

- **Hide.** Take a look at how well this works in schools. Teachers cluster 20 or more students into small rooms or closets, making it like shooting fish in a barrel for the attacker. In cases where hiding is the only option, you should have predetermined hiding places which only a few people share—ideally with a door that locks. The harder it is to find you, the more time the rampage attacker has to look for victims and the less time he has to execute the attack. If you cannot find cover, hit the deck. The military doesn't teach their personnel to curl up in a ball and wait to get shot, they order them to hit the ground and lay flat and still. This is especially effective in a rampage attack where you are likely to either appear dead or where you will not be seen as a threat to the attacker.

- Jonathan Gold shares my unease at the advice to hide, "This assumes that the person will choose a hiding place that is bullet proof. If the gunman has an AR15 you don't stand much of a chance if you are armed with a heavy hole punch or stapler."

- **Fight back.** If the American penal system has taught us anything, it's that virtually anything can be utilized[77] as a

---

[77] *I hate people who misuse the word "utilize" as synonymous with the word "use." Utilize means to find utility in, in other words put something to a use that it was not initially intended.*

weapon. Something heavy, sharp, pointed, or caustic is probably nearby, so know exactly how you're going to arm yourself BEFORE the rampage attack is underway. DON"T have a gun, each of my knowledgeable sources told me (off the record) that they are going to "take out" anyone with a gun, because it is impossible to tell whether the person is actually a "friendly" or an attacker. They will kill them all and let God sort them out, but they aren't going to say that publicly.

Many people—even law enforcement personnel—advocate allowing people to arm themselves with firearms (provided that they have the appropriate permits and training.) Andrew Arena disagrees, " I am a gun owner and support gun ownership. However, more guns in a building does not always lead to increased safety. The level of training is all over the board."

A New Model

Andrew Arena opines that "Run, hide, fight" is obviously the 'go to' training model today. It is one that I use, but not in a vacuum. The major issue with this theory is that it is not an absolute continuum and should be taught as 'options' when faced with an active shooter. There are so many unknowns in each situation, such as, are there additional shooters? Where are they located? Etc. The facts of each situation will lead the options pursued. We teach employees to identify the situation they are facing and know their surroundings. Train and think about it before it happens."

After conversations with Andrew Arena, Jonathan Gold, and other experts, I developed the following, more practical approach: Expect, Prepare, Assess, Alert, Evacuate, Take Cover, and (absolutely as a last resort) Attack.

- **Expect.** The greatest advantage the rampage killer has is the element of surprise; you need to take that away from him. This book has armed you with the skills to spot the situations and circumstances that are conducive to a rampage attack. Treat it with the same preparedness and diligence that you do a fire. Ask yourself what you would do if you founc yourseelf amidst a rampage attack.

Expecting an attack will help you stay in control of yourself and of the situation. Rampage attackers often enjoy and feed on chaos, an apparently empty area isn't an attractive hunting ground. The rampage killer is more likely to move on than to waste precious seconds playing hide and seek. From the moment the rampage starts, the attacker is on the clock and time is the enemy. Expecting an attack cuts cown the amount of time a rampage attacker has to kill people. According to Jonathan Gold, "The best way to avoid being a target is to be prepared in advance," but he is quick to add, "we better be prepared to improvise."

- **Prepare.** Know the evacuation routes and the quickest way to get to the nearest one. "Look for less obvious places where you can seek cover and if you can't get out, find a good hiding place," says Andrew Arena. You should know where you are going to hide BEFORE an attacker is on the premises. Jonathan Gold agrees, "The plan before the attack is almost more important than the actions you take during the attack," he says.Gold takes it one step further, belying his past as a private detective and the fact that he was shot on the job, "Every building I enter I find the quickest route to safety and I walk [it] each day." And—as silly as it may seem to some— "Drill every day."

- **Assess.** Before deciding on a course of action, it's important to do a quick assessment. Most of my expert sources agree that you can't just have a one-size-fits all approach to rampage attacks. So when things move from theoretical danger to actual danger, you can move seamlessly to "plan B."

- **Alert.** As soon as you suspect a rampage attack is, or is about to be, underway, pull the fire alarm. This is a far more effective way of getting an emergency response to your location. The sirens rapidly descending on the scene may send the rampage attacker into a panic, causing him to flee. But that doesn't mean that the police don't need to be notified. After you have found a safe place, send a group text to your family and friends telling them to notify 911 immediately. Text (silently, don't use talk to text) the presence of an armed intruder and your exact location. Next, turn the volume all the way down on your phone and call 911 and slowly put the phone down, leaving the line open; this way emergency responders can hear what's going on and, in some cases, have a better chance of quickly reaching the location.

- **Evacuate.** If the rampage attacker has not yet reached your location, follow basic fire drill rules for evacuating the building. Stop what you're doing, turn off your phone's ringer, and silently walk—not run—to the evacuation route. Find cover and get out of sight. Once an all clear signal is given, go to your rally point, but it is of the utmost importance that you NOT go to the rally point until AFTER the police declare the scene "all clear."

- **Take Cover.** If the rampage attacker is already on the scene, go to the nearest room that has no windows and a door that can be locked. Watch for other employees headed your way and continue to quickly get as many coworkers into the room as possible before closing and locking the door. Once the door is closed and locked, do not reopen it until an all clear signal has sounded. If the door cannot be locked, quickly place furniture in front of it. If the attacker tries to enter the room, wait until he is partially in the room before throwing the entire weight of your body against the door, ideally causing significant injury and disabling the attacker. Turn off the light if you are able to do so. If you reach the room once it has been locked, move to your secondary hiding spot. Do not panic, scream, cry, or pound on the door. Move stealthily to a spot that is outside the line of vision, ideally behind shelves, file cabinets, or something else durable enough to lessen a bullet penetrating it.

- **Attack, but only as a last resort.** In this case you may well be terrified, and when you are terrified you are likely to behave irrationally and do exactly what the armed person tells you. So it's easy to say, "I'm not going to sit there and wait to be killed," but that's exactly what a lot of people do. If you are able to do so, remain calm. Remember, before fleeing to your hiding spot grab a pair of scissors or any of the office supplies that can be used as a weapon. If you are discovered by the gunman, don't engage with him. Recently an asshat said you should smile and say something like, "Hi, I think we went to high school together." This is a surefire way to get yourself killed (as you have essentially told the attacker that you can identify him.) Don't try to bargain with the attacker, instead use the scissors to stab him in the eye, ribcage, or underarm. You may lose that fight, but you will cost the shooter time that he can't afford to lose. Remember, this is the last resort, so don't try to be a hero and don't go on the offensive unless you have truly no other choice. Heroes make the news, but people who tried to be a hero and failed are just dead.

Jonathan Gold sums things up nicely, (during a rampage attack) "Do whatever it takes to make yourself not the target."

Remember, the rampaging attacker may have a gun, but you have the home field advantage. Rampage killer events are often over long before the police arrive, so the attackers tend to strike quickly and either flee or kill themselves. It may seem like hours, but the average event is typically measured in only minutes.

Dealing with Police/First Responders

If you were able to get out of the kill zone, you may have to help the first responders by answering:

- Is the shooter still on the premises?

- Who is the shooter?

- What does the shooter look like?

- With what is the shooter armed?

- When did the event start?

- Who is the target?

- Where on the premises is the shooter (if you know) or where are the victims?

- Approximately how many injured are there?

You will likely be in shock or another highly emotional state. Your coworkers and friends need you to stay calm and be as lucid as you can be. Practice talking to first responders during drills and in the event of an attack, try to gather as much information as you possibly can while you wait for the first responders.

Summary

The chance that you will be present at a rampage attack is infinitesimally small, and yet there is a chance. That's why people buy lottery tickets even though the odds of winning are so incredibly against them. If you are unfortunate enough to be on-site during a rampage attack, it is important to try to remain calm and to remember that while the rampage attacker has the element of surprise, his time is limited and the attack will be over in a matter of minutes. By following the basic process of Expect, Prepare, Alert, Evacuate, Take Cover, and (when necessary) Attack, you greatly increase your chances of surviving unharmed.

Thought Starters

How would you prepare for a potential rampage attack?

Why is the "run, hide, fight back" response to a rampage attack dangerous and outdated?

Why is a resilient culture safer than a non- or low-resilience organization?

Why is providing accurate information to law enforcement essential?

Stop. Don't Shoot!

Chapter 15: You Can Stop the Violence

I started writing this book over two years ago, before the pandemic and before all the madness. It was depressing to write and I almost quit. Were it not for the urging of my publicist and publisher, this book would likely never come into fruition. There's no denying that this isn't exactly an uplifting read, but we have to talk about the issues covered in this book, not the least of which being domestic violence.

Every day that we ignore the red flags, every day that we ignore signs of domestic violence or violence in the home, we perpetuate the underlying causes of mass violence. But take heart; there's still hope. Your creepy coworker probably won't go on a killing spree, and your ex probably won't try to kill you. But consider the long odds of the lottery; while it probably won't happen to you, millions of people still buy lottery tickets. And always remember that while the rampage attacker has the advantage of surprise, you have the home field advantage. The best news though is that there are things you can do to protect yourself and others:

1. Never ignore the signs of domestic violence, mental illness, or substance abuse.

2. If you see something suspicious in the behavior of someone, ask them if everything is okay. They might tell you to mind your own business, but IT IS YOUR BUSINESS!!

3. Intervene early.

4. Forewarned is forearmed. Now that you have read this, take the time to look around your workplace, shopping malls, and concert venues (anyplace that would be an attractive target—you need to think like a rampage killer) and:

   a. Determine your escape route.

   b. Determine an alternative escape route.

   c. Preprogram the numbers for internal security, 911(including the numbers required to access an outside line,) and Human Resources into your desk or cell phone.

   d. Identify the closest secure hiding place.

   e. Identify a makeshift weapon (like a pair of scissors or a heavy lamp) that you can easily take with you as you evacuate. In a public venue, carry something that can be used as a weapon but that security won't forbid you to take in (like a cane or an umbrella.)

   f. In public venues, be sure not to bunch up in a crowd. If the evacuation is chaotic, hit the ground (choose a spot that will prevent you from being trampled.)

5. Familiarize yourself with your company's or venue's policies regarding workplace violence.

6. Remind others to obey the rules designed to protect you.

7. Alert Human Resources or security of erratic behavior of coworkers or other patrons in a public venue.

8. Flee dangerous situations early, ideally before the violence starts; better safe than sorry and better safe than dead.

9. Don't panic. You got this.

Stop. Don't Shoot!

Chapter 16: Conclusion

This is less of a conclusion than a call to action. We need to wake up and take action. When I was promoting *Lone Gunman Rewriting the Handbook of Workforce Violence Prevention,* I was horrified to learn that on average, men would doubt the statistics of violence against women and women would look at me sadly and say, "yeah, nobody cares about violence against women."

Well, I care. I have a wonderful wife and three daughters (one biological, one step-daughter, and one stolen (who to this day calls me half-dad.) I have three beautiful, delightful granddaughters, three nieces, a deceased mother, two great nieces, and countless family members who are women (or God willing, someday will be) and I love them and want nothing but good things for them.

And if after reading this book and seeing the connection between violence in the home (typically against women) you don't care, I don't know what to say except I genuinely feel sorry for you and the women in your life.

If you are feeling helpless, don't. We are not helpless and we can do things to stop this cycle:

- Make it clear to your children that violence is only acceptable in self-defense, and self-defense means that you are genuinely in fear that you are in imminent danger and cannot flee the situation.

- Instead of fighting, photograph or videotape the aggressor (and if they are in a vehicle, photograph their license plate.) Notify the police of the assault (legally if someone threatens you with violence and you have a reasonable expectation that they can commit the violence it is an assault it's a crime.)

- Tell everyone you know how to spot an abusive partner and how to get out before they are in too deep. Abusers can be very convincing with their apologies and promises that they will "never do it again, sorry," but they will escalate the violence until things end in tragedy.

- Call your politicians and make them aware of your feelings about rampage attacks and the need for a better approach to mental illness and domestic violence.

We can only end this problem by caring about it and talking about it. But more so, each one of us needs to become a private activist against violence in the home.

About The Author:

Photo credit: D'Jorge Tomás

Phil La Duke is a popular speaker & writer with more than 2,500 works in print. He has contributed to *Authority*, Buzzfeed, *Entrepreneur*, Monster, Thrive Global, and many more works and is published on all inhabited continents. He is the author of four books and a contributor to one more. His first book is a visceral, no-holds-barred look at worker safety, *I Know My Shoes Are Untied! Mind Your Own Business. An Iconoclast's View of Workers' Safety*. His second book *Lone Gunman: Rewriting the Handbook On Workplace Violence Prevention* which deals with workplace violence, particularly directed at women, is listed as #16 on *Pretty Progressive* magazine's list of 49 Books that Powerful Women Study in Detail. His third book, *Blood In My Pockets Is Blood On Your Hands,* is a powerful look at the consequences of "Zero Injury" campaigns. *Stop. Don't Shoot!* was painstakingly researched both through reviewing studies dealing with mass shootings and interviews with experts and gun owner advocates. Next up will be an updated version of *Lone Gunman: Rewriting the Handbook On Workplace Violence Prevention*, followed by *Loving An Addict: Collateral Damage Of the Opioid Epidemic* due to be released in 2023. La Duke also contributed a chapter of 1% Safer, a not-for-profit book written by the

"top game-changers and global thought leaders." Phil is listed in the top 20 experts in the Future of Work and about 25 other disciplines by Expert File.

In addition to his extensive writing, La Duke is currently employed as a Business Consultant and a Production Safety Consultant for the film and television industries.

Follow Phil
Twitter: @philladuke
Facebook: https://www.facebook.com/booksarticlesravingsandrantings
Weekly blog www.philladuke.wordpress.com

About the Experts with Whom I Consulted

Andrew Arena

Andrew G. Arena obtained a Bachelor of Science at Central Michigan University and did graduate work in England at Cambridge University. He received his Juris Doctorate from the University of Detroit School of Law.

Mr. Arena joined the FBI as a special agent in June 1988. He rose through the rank and ultimately was promoted to chief of the International Terrorism Operations Section at FBI Headquarters. The following year, he was appointed special assistant to the executive assistant director for counterterrorism and counterintelligence and assigned to the Director's office, soon afterward Director Robert S. Mueller, III promoted Mr. Arena to the position of special agent in charge of the New York Division. Mr. Arena was in charge of all criminal investigations in the New York office.

Andrew G. Arena spent 24 years with the FBI, and perhaps must notably as the Chief of International Terrorism Operations at FBI headquarters after the 9-11 attacks. When he left the FBI he was Special Agent in Charge, Detroit Field Office and he is now Executive Director, Detroit Crime Commission and the founder of A.S. Consulting, LLC. If you are thinking that Director of a Crime Commission sounds like Charlie "Lucky" Luciano's job title, you're not alone; I thought the same thing, but in fact Mr. Arena is actually working on the side of the law and is not a reputed, alleged, or actual leader of a national crime syndicate. His firm, A.S. Consulting, is a highly respected, specialized consultancy that teaches companies how to protect themselves from rampage attacks. It's fair to describe Mr. Arena as a definitive source of knowledge on terrorism—domestic and international. If I were to hire someone to speak to my organization about mass shootings (assuming I wasn't available) I would recommend A.S Consulting.

Jonathan Gold

Jonathan Gold is a 43 year resident of the state of Michigan. He attended University of Michigan- Dearborn and the Miami University of Ohio. Mr. Gold is a NRA trained private pistol and gun safety instructor who has logged over 1,000 hours of training aside from teaching and is a registered lifetime member of the NRA despite his attempts to resign. He is the Michigan Chapter President of Giffords Gun Owners for Safety.

Jonathan Gold is a devoted advocate for gun ownership but also an outspoken critic of irresponsible gun ownership.

Gold's impressive knowledge of guns and gun violence made much of this book not only relevant, but also possible.

A gunshot survivor himself, Mr. Gold is living proof that one need not oppose the ownership of guns to be anti-gun violence.

I owe both these gentlemen, and the many researchers who published studies in highly respected journals, a great deal of appreciation.

Made in the USA
Columbia, SC
08 January 2023

75641651R00143